AMERICAN CHURCHES AND SOUTHERN AFRICA

Rhetoric and Reality

Columba Aham Nnorom

University Press of America, Inc.
Lanham • New York • London

Copyright © 1997 by
University Press of America,® Inc.
4720 Boston Way
Lanham, Maryland 20706

3 Henrietta Street
London, WC2E 8LU England

Library of Congress Cataloging-in-Publication Data

Nnorom, Columba, Aham.
American churches and Southern Africa, rhetoric and reality / by
Reverend Columba Aham Nnorom.
p.   cm.
Includes bibliographical references.
l. Africa, Southern--Foreign relations--United States. 2. United
States--Foreign relations--Africa, Southern. 3. Christianity and
international affairs. 4. Race relations--Religious aspects--Christianity.
5. Africa, Southern--Race relations. 6. United States--Race relations.
I. Title.
DT1105.U6N66   1996   327.73068--dc20   96-35235 CIP

ISBN 0-7618-0567-2 (cloth : alk. ppr.)

CONTENTS

ACKNOWLEDGEMENTS

It is impossible to thank everybody who helped to make the writing of this book a reality. First, I would like to express my heartfelt gratitude to Professor Ronald Walters, chairman of the Political Science Department of Howard University, for reading the manuscript and for letting me benefit from his vast knowledge of African and American politics. Second, I would also like to thank Drs. Nikolas A. Starrou, Mar King, Henry Ferry, Vincent Browne, Michael Nwanze, and Kunirum Osia, for their support and insight.

Third, this book would never have been written but for the invaluable cooperation and indefatigable interest of several American church groups. In this regard, I am grateful to a friend and mentor, Rev. Edgar Lockwood, former director of the Washington Office on Africa; to Dr. Warren Willis, the archivist at the United States Catholic Conference; Rev. Rawlings Lambert, formerly of the USCC; Rev. Robert Brooks of the Washington Office of the Episcopal Church, L. Robert McClean of the UMC; Sister Catherine Pinkerton of Network; Bob Dumas of the Africa Division, Justice and Peace Committee of the USCC; Canons Kwasi Thornell and Michael Hamilton of the Washington Cathedral; Gretchen Eick of IMPACT; Andrea Young of UCC; and Tom Bailey, Kenneth Martin, Jerry Herman of the Society of Friends (Quakers).

Thank you, Drs. John Ukawuilulu and Charles Iheagwara, dear and beloved friends, for consistenly and relentlessly challenging this author to get this book finished and published.

Finally, I would like to express my gratitude to Ms. Kimberly A. Turner for typing and retyping this book.

FOREWORD

It is an honor to commend this book to the attention of readers who are concerned about the future of Africa and the role of the Christian church in Africa.

When Father Columba Nnorom arrived on my doorstep several years ago, it was a moment to treasure. He was completing his doctorate at Howard University and I was the former director of the Washington Office on Africa, full of memories which I was eager to share. We sat and talked for four hours straight. It was a joyful feast.

As far as I am aware, his book is the first to explore the engagement of the churches in the struggle for freedom and de-colonization in Southern Africa in the 1960-1990 period. His focus is on our attempts to influence public policy, particularly in the area of legislation. He comes at his task with scholarly rigor and with the passion of a Pan-Africanist. He is particularly critical of the torpor and apathy of the churches in the face of white supremacy and settler colonialism. The churches were by and large collaborators in those systemic injustices.

Father Nnorom is right to raise these issues, which should profoundly trouble us all. As someone who participated in the legislative campaigns of the 1970's, I can only say that I am amazed at what we accomplished given what has come later. The challenges of genocidal conflict in Rwanda and dictatorial misrule in Nigeria cannot be taken off our agenda. Nor can aid to the newly independent states, provided it is the right kind of aid. The temptation to write Africa off once more as a hopeless course of a uniquely "dark" continent beyond redemption is with us today but it must be vigorously resisted.

Father Nnorom is right to call us to account for our moral lassitude. All of us have participated in it. Nevertheless, we can take encouragement from what we did accomplish. Apartheid is ended. The Portuguese colonial system is finished. Enormous problems, political and economic face the newly independent states. We cannot abandon our concern for peacemaking, reconstruction and development now.

I would hope that this book will serve as a reminder of the accomplishments as well as the shortcomings of our efforts to bring about liberation in Southern Africa. It deserves to be widely read.

The Rev. Edgar Lockwood
Former Director, Washington Office on Africa
Advent IV, 1995
Falmouth, Ma. 02540

CHAPTER I - Introduction

NATURE AND STATEMENT OF THE PROBLEM

Southern Africa, that region of Africa that runs from "Mozambique around the Cape of Good Hope up to Angola,"[0] is a land of contrasts. On the one hand, it embraces an area blessed with a temperate climate and disproportionate deposits of strategic minerals that has earned it the title, "the Persian Gulf of minerals."[1] On the other hand, it is a region plagued by centuries of war between blacks and whites, political instability, and a degree of inter-racial violence unknown in any other region of Africa.

Unlike the rest of the continent, southern Africa was partially by-passed by the independence "revolution" sweeping Africa in the late 1950s and early 1960s. In Rhodesia, Ian Smith and a minority group of white settlers adopted a Unilateral Declaration of Independence (UDI) in 1965 rather than hand over power to the black majority. Indeed, Rhodesia did become independent Zimbabwe in 1980, but only after multi-nation negotiations. While the Lancaster negotiations, called to find a solution to the Rhodesian crisis, may have led to the transfer of political power to the African majority, it created other problems for the new government, especially in the economic sphere. Thus, ten years after Zimbabwe's independence, the Mugabe government has been unable to expedite action on a full-scale land redistribution program due to constraints placed on it by the pre-independence agreements. There were, however, other extenuating factors.

In Angola and Mozambique, over four centuries of Portuguese colonialism ended only in the mid-1970's to be replaced by the African nationalist governments of the Movimento Popular de Libertacao de Angola (Popular Movement for the Liberation of Angola - MPLA) and the Mozambique Liberation Front (FRELIMO), respectively. Both countries are, however, still faced with serious threats posed by two reactionary guerrilla groups. In Angola, earlier hopes that the September 1992, democratic elections would bring to an end the country's civil war have been dashed. For after losing the UN-supervised elections, UNITA accused its rival, the MPLA, of massive rigging. UNITA radio "Voice of the Cockerel" claimed that since it had outpolled its opponent in rival UNITA strongholds, "the majority of the Angolan people have sought a definitive change of regime".[2] However, the recognition of the fairness of Angola's

first experiment in multi-party elections was recognized by the U.S. and other impartial observers. UNITA's recent failure to seize Luanda after the loss of its top commanders, and the international pressure for a negotiated settlement, may have forced the rebel leadership to reconsider. On December 9, 1992, UNITA decided to join "a government of national unity and include its forces in a new unified army..."[3] But it is still doubtful whether UNITA leader, Jonas Savimbi, will keep his word this time.

In Mozambique, after a sixteen-year civil war, the Mozambique Liberation Front (FRELIMO) and the Mozambique National Resistance (MNR or RENEMO) signed a ceasefire in Rome on October 4, 1992.[4] Brokered by two Catholic priests and a lay historian, the fifty-page agreement establishes a ceasefire, the creation of a single army from the forces of RENAMO and the FRELIMO-led government in Maputo, the presence of a U.N. commission to oversee the creation of political parties, and the holding of free election in one years time.[5]

On March 21, 1990, after decades of armed struggle against South African occupation, SWAPO led Namibia to independence. Like Zimbabwe, Namibia's independence was a product of multinational negotiations. But, unlike Zimbabwe, its transition to independence was supervised by the United Nations. It is, however, the author's considered opinion that while the negotiated settlements of both Zimbabwean and Namibian wars helped to save lives, it also moderated the revolutionary effects of both struggles. In the former, it led to the postponement of the distribution of some of the economic rewards that would have come with independence. The same could happen in the latter. The danger of the cooptation of the South African struggle in the same manner is very real.

In South Africa, however, the situation has remained virtually unchanged for centuries. Ever since the Dutch arrived at the Cape in 1652 where they found the Khoikhoi (men of men) people a prosperous and organized community[6], the plight of the African population has deteriorated. From 1774-1793, the Dutch perpetrated a "quiet holocaust" against the African population.[7] By a series of coordinated commando raids, they sought to wipe out the Khoikhoi people by exterminating the male population and by dividing the women and children as booty.[8] Like some Australian aborigine and American-Indian groups, the Khoikhoi are today a virtually extinct African people.[9] The discovery of gold and diamonds in South Africa in the 19th century led to an influx of Europeans to the region and the increased deprivation of the Africans of their land and property. However, it was the rise of the Afrikaner nationalist power in 1948 and the declaration of apartheid as the official policy of South African government, that entrenched white minority power and its subjugation of the African majority in South Africa.

Unfortunately, Pretoria's ambitions extended beyond its borders. Ever since the independence of Angola (1975), Mozambique (1974) and Zimbabwe (1980), she has launched a campaign of destabilization against its young and vulnerable neighbors. The human and material cost of this campaign is immense. According to UNICEF, by the end of 1988, "a child under the age of five was dying every 3.5 minutes in Mozambique and Angola, 17 every hour, 408 everyday, equivalent to a jumbo jet filled with children crashing everyday,"[10] Angola, a country of only 10 million people, has the largest number (40,000) of limbless people per capita in the world.[11] In 1988, the U.S. State Department called RENAMO's attacks in Mozambique "a systematic and brutal war of terror against innocent civilians through forced labor, starvation, physical abuse and wanton killing, one of the most brutal holocausts against ordinary human beings since the second world war,"[12] and costing over $60 billion and 1.5 million lives since 1980.[13]

South Africa's policy of apartheid, which is responsible for such enormous human suffering, has been condemned as a "crime against humanity"[14] and as "abhorrent" to the human conscience. It has reduced Pretoria to the status of a pariah state, "a skunk among nations."[15]

But international opprobrium for the racist regime in South Africa could not resolve the problems of the region. For as long as South Africa remained under the clutches of apartheid, political stability and economic prosperity continued to elude the region. Jesse Jackson was right:

   The heart of apartheid was in Pretoria but its tentacles were in the region.[16]

        Consequently, apartheid South Africa stood impregnable for decades inspite of internal and international pressure. It seemed to have outlived the predictions of analysts who saw its collapse as imminent. As Pretoria's dirty tricks encouraged and exacerbated inter-ethnic violence that led to the slaughter of thousands of Africans in the late 1980's to the early 1990's, South African leaders exuded confidence while holding firm to the evil apartheid apparatus. De Klerk once told a western diplomat: "Don't expect me to negotiate myself out of office."[10] Mr. Botha South Africa's former foreign minister wondered why Pretoria should "surrender when we have not been defeated."[11]

    But the white minority regime which had survived the wind of change sweeping through Africa in the 1960's could not withstand the collapse of communism and the rebirth of democracy in Eastern Europe and the former Soviet Union in the late 1980's. Soon cracks began to appear in apartheid laager as Pretoria began a genuine attempt to dismantle white minority rule. With the lifting of the ban on the ANC and the thirty three opposition groups(Feb. 2, 1990), the release of Nelson Mandela from the Victor Vester Prison after twenty-seven years of imprisonment(Feb. 2, 1990) and the release of Walter Sisulu and six other ANC activists(Oct. 15, 1990)[12] the march toward black majority rule accelerated. It ended with "Fifteen days that shook the world: from the holding of the first all race election in South Africa from April 26 - May 2, 1994 to the installation of "Madiba"(Mandela), as his countrymen call him on May 10, 1994[13] as South Africa's first black president. These momentous events were preceeded by a gruelling four years of negotiations during which new constitution was adopted and a Transitional Executive Team chosen. According to Sparks, the South African election signalled the end of an era: "In historical terms it might even be said to bring to a close an era that began when the Portuguese navigator, Bartholomew Dias, nudged his little caravelle nervously across the equator 500 years ago to reach the Cape of Good Hope and so opened the western seaway to the East, and with that the age of colonialism with all its assumptions of racial superiority and the white man's burden."[14]

    No direct political links existed between the U.S. and

southern Africa until 1779, when the young American revolutionary government, desperate for international recognition, established diplomatic relations with the white settlers at the Cape.[17] Traditionally, the strategic interest of the U.S. in the region centers on the Republic of South Africa and is based on three critical stakes: a corporate stake that is due to the over concentration of American companies in South Africa; an "economic and strategic" stake that demands the protection of the Cape route used by Western European and U.S.-bound ships carrying petroleum and non-fuel minerals to their dependent industries, and a "security interest" that arises out of the fear that a racial blood-bath, caused by Pretoria's policy of apartheid, could drag the U.S. into an African race war.[18]

American's interests in southern Africa are also moral and humanitarian and, therefore, pose a foreign policy dilemma. According to Henry Jackson,

> South Africa poses a challenge to political rationality as well as a test of national morality, because the racial situation there, more than anywhere else in the world, impinges directly on American security.... Nowhere else does an area of American foreign policy so directly call into question and threaten to inflame racial tensions at home.[19]

Ross Baker has identified five main American groups interested in African issues: The Africanists (professionals), missionary-oriented and humanitarian groups (sentimentalists), businessmen (entrepreneurs), and apartheid exponents (irreconcilables).[20] Other groups ignored by Baker are military, strategic and government bureaucratic interests. American missionary and humanitarian groups interested in Africa are drawn primarily from Catholic and Protestant churches. Traditionally, they have played a minor and limited but positive role in the shaping of U.S. African policy. This is borne out by the fact that in those cases where they have sought to influence U.S. policy on African issues, American churches have generally succeeded in bringing about cosmetic rather than substantive change. For example, during the Nigeria-Biafra War (1967-1970), American church groups were instrumental in the decision of both the Johnson and Nixon administrations to send humanitarian aid to Nigeria and Biafra[21] and in the holding of congressional hearings on Biafra by senators Edward Kennedy and Eugene McCarthy.[22] Nonetheless, in spite of the efforts of some churches, the pro-Nigeria policy of the U.S. government remained unchanged.[23]

Bellah and Brill have identified "two important moments" of significant church influence in the shaping of U.S. foreign policy. The first was during the "evangelical revival or second awakening" of the early 19th century when America maintained a low military and political profile worldwide, while its missionaries transmitted American values to the world.[24] The second was the "moment of social responsibility," when the churches resolved that the structural problems of poverty and justice at home must go hand in hand with efforts to bring justice and equality to the world.[25] In southern Africa, while the attempts of American churches to confront the problems of colonialism and racism are broadly analyzed in the context of their passive and activist phases, their actual efforts to influence U.S. policy per se may be divided into three distinct periods: 1) Near total consensus on U.S. support for European colonialism and Boer settler supremacy in southern Africa (1834-1948); 2) Opposition to U.S. policy and support for absolute non-violent tactics to resolve the colonial and racial problems in southern Africa (1949-1959); 3) Opposition to U.S. policy and qualified support for the use of armed violence to redress the racial inequalities in southern Africa (1960-1986).

The period of near-total consensus of American church groups in their support of U.S. southern Africa policy may be traced to the formation in 1810 of the American Board of Commissioners, an interdenominational white protestant group, and the sending of missionaries to South Africa (1834), Angola (1880), and Rhodesia (1893).[26] During this period, American missionaries in southern Africa were almost in total support of the U.S. government in its pro-European and pro-Boer colonial domination of the Africans. In fact, unlike some European missionaries who gave arms to the Africans to defend themselves against the Boers[27], they had no qualms accepting from Cecil Rhodes, the doyen of British imperialism in southern Africa, land violently taken from the Africans[28] to establish their missions. The cooperation between these white missionaries and the Europeans as well as the Boers was so total that it was an American missionary who gave a copy of the American constitution to the latter on which they based their Volksroad (elected assembly).[29] The Boers denied the franchise to the African majority just as the original American constitution denied it to the African-American minority in the U.S.

However, in spite of the collusion of most American

missionaries with European and Boer domination of southern Africa, there were still pockets of "proto-opposition" to white supremacy among them and those they came to evangelize. This opposition could be traced to the emergence of Ethiopianism in South Africa and the important connections it established with African-American churches in the U.S. Ethiopianism, which arose out of the desire of the Africans "to be somebody, ...to initiate, to enjoy the sense of proprietorship in homestead, business, school and church"[30] traces its origin to a situation not unlike that of the American Methodist Episcopal church (AME) about a century earlier.[31] It started with the founding of the first South-African church in the 1870's. By 1892, that relationship had been strengthened by the establishment of the first Ethiopian church in Pretoria.[32] Its founder, Rev. M.M. Makone, an African minister of the white-controlled Wesleyan Methodist church, had broken away from that church because of racism. He was later joined by Dwane, another Wesleyan minister, who was sent to the U.S. in 1893 to negotiate the affiliation of the Ethiopian church with the AME church.[33]

The merger of both churches set in motion a chain reaction of events and contacts within South Africa and in the U.S. whose reverberations are still being felt today in the anti-apartheid movement in both countries. Bishop Turner, who visited South Africa in 1898, represents some of the immediate benefits of the Ethiopia-AME church connection and the more progressive approach of the American denomination to the anti-colonial struggle in southern Africa. On the religious plane, he praised the Ethiopian spirit that had led black South Africans to "discover that churches of their own race would be of far more benefit in a pragmatic measure than worshipping among whites, where they are compelled to occupy a subordinate status."[34] Consequently, he ordained as AME church ministers thirty-one elders and twenty deacons and promoted Rev. Dwane from superintendent to vicar bishop of the South African district of the church.[35] On the political plane, he was more cautious and conciliatory. He visited Paul Kruger, the Afrikaner president of Transvaal, who conceded that "you are the first black man whose hand I have ever shaken."[36] In his public speeches, he hid his political inclinations and seemed to blame black South Africans rather than the colonial system that oppressed them.[37]

But before private and all-black congregations, the real Bishop Turner emerged. It was Turner, the "arch-critic of U.S. imperialism and racism and an outspoken emigrationist," who advocates the "need for the international solidarity of blacks, the efficacy of assertive and concerted action to redress their common grievances, and the necessity for defensive violence."[38] It was also the Turner who refused to obey South Africa's segregation laws but "travelled, lived, and ate wherever he wished without incident."[39] By promoting the unity of the Ethiopian and AME churches and by identifying the suffering of black South Africans with those of blacks in the U.S., Turner played a leading role in the promotion of Evangelical Pan Africanism[40] and "proto-opposition" to European colonialism by an American church group.

Another benefit of the AME church connection to South Africa was the relationship developed between many African students and visitors in the U.S. The connections made by such South African students like Sol Plaatje,[41] Dube and Pixley with black American pan-Africanists such as Garvey and Dubois,[42] and organizations like the NAACP, helped to keep the torch of anti-colonialism alive in southern Africa. For example, the NAACP, which was founded in 1909 played a role in the formation of the ANC in 1912.[43]

John Chilembwe also represents the impact of the anti-colonial Pan-African spirit promoted by some African-American missionaries and some of the worst nightmares of European colonialism. He was converted to christianity and sent to the U.S. by Joseph Booth, a John Brown-type English missionary. Booth was a pan-Africanist who had promoted a scheme called the African Christian Union, "an idea to involve all of African extraction the world over to unite in the organization of a semi-benevolent joint stock company for the commercial occupation of Africa."[44] Like Garvey, he advocated economic pan-Africanism.

> Let the African be his own employer, develop his own country, establish his own manufactures, run his own ship, work his own mines, and conserve the wealth from his labor for his God-given land for the upliftment of the people and the glory of God. Let the call be long and loud and clear to everyone with African blood coursing in his veins... Africa for the Africans.

Joseph Booth was deported from Africa on several occasions because of his progressive views on racial equality. After Chilenbwe's education in an African-American university and ordination as a minister, he parted company with his mentor and allied himself with his African-American friends. With their support, he set up a mission in present day Malawi to educate his people in the arts, crafts and christianity." In 1915, this African freedom fighter and Nat Turner-like figure led a small army against the colonial order killing three whites, wounding others, and, at least, momentarily, threatening to stem the growth of the settler presence in southern Africa.[45]

All the same, the actual impact of the Ethiopia-AME church connection should not be overexaggerated. Many African-American missionaries in southern Africa were rather conservative in their challenge to white supremacy. Many of them believed that imperialism was necessary to "civilize" and unite the Africans. Moreover, the white colonist also gave them certain special privileges, which racism had denied them in America.[46] Dwane, who became an AME church bishop severed his connection with the church because most African-American parishes preferred light-skinned ministers to dark-skinned ones.[47]

The real and imagined activism by African-American missionaries on southern African led to a white backlash. Thus, not only were some privileges taken away from AME church ministers, the church was also banned in some parts of the region.[48] There was fear within the white community that under AME church's influence, Africans now looked to their African-American cousins rather than to their traditional liberal white allies for guidance and inspiration.[49] They were also afraid that unless this incipient relationship was "nipped in the bud," it could foment an African revolution against the colonial system.

In 1884, when American protestants sent their first missionaries to southern Africa, U.S. Catholics were battling nativism and other forms of anti-Catholic prejudice.[50] As a missionary church that ceased to be under direct supervision of the Vatican only in 1908,[51] American Catholics were not an important factor in the early U.S. cultural penetration of southern Africa. It was not until 1841 that the first American Catholic missionaries were sent to sub-Saharan Africa to take care of Catholics among the 3,000 African-Americans repatriated to Liberia.[52] One of the priests, Edward Barron, became the first bishop in 1842 in a territory running from Senegal to the Orange Free State in present day South Africa.[53] Generally, American catholic missionaries in the 19th century who were virtually all-white, were no less supportive of European colonialism than were their white protestant counterparts.

The emergence of Afrikaner power and the declaration of apartheid as official policy of the South African government in 1948 marked a new stage in the efforts of American church groups to influence U.S. policy towards southern Africa. In the same year, the World Council of

Churches (WCC), which was to play an important global role in the anti-colonial struggle in Africa, was founded. In the U.S., the churches began to use their global connections to mount organized opposition to U.S. southern Africa Policy[54] while at the same time, advocating absolute non-violent tactics to resolve the racist problems of the region. These churches were "predominantly protestant, pacifist and white," the most active being the Episcopal church, the United Church of Christ and the Methodist church.[55]

Nonetheless, the anti-colonial struggle in southern Africa was not a monopoly of the churches during this period. For example, on June 19, 1946, the Council on African Affairs (CAA), which was founded by Paul Robeson and the African-American sociologist Max Yergan, called a massive rally attended by 15,000 people in Madison Square Garden, to denounce the racist regime in South Africa and to oppose plans for the annexation of Namibia by South Africa.[56] In the same year, the CAA "hosted the first delegation of the South African Liberation Movement to the United Nations."[57] In 1953, a group of former missionaries and government officials founded the African-American Institute dedicated to influencing U.S. Policy toward Africa.[58]

As the "midwife" of 15th and 16th century European colonialism,[59] the Catholic church has traditionally been hamstrung in its ability to give its full support to the anti-colonial struggle in Africa. This was especially the case with those colonies governed by Spain and Portugal, two "catholic" countries with whom the church has traditionally nurtured a special relationship. In Angola and Mozambique, for example, the church lent its support to Portuguese colonialism because it promoted evangelization.[60] During this period, papal bulls, such as Apostolicae Dignitatis Specula, Eximia Devotionis (1420), Aeteri Regis Aementia (1480), and Eaque Pro Bono Pacis encouraged European colonists in their conquest of Africa.[61]

> The right of the Crown of Portugal to the sovereignty of the lands of discovery was explicitly recognized in papal bull of 1452 and this right was confirmed by the bull of Pope Julius II in 1506, which ratified the Treaty of Tordesillas. Therein it was stated that those lands should remain and belong to the King of Portugal and his successors forever and ever.[62]

However, the modern colonial relationship between the Catholic church and Portuguese colonialism in Africa is based on the

Concordant signed by Pope Pius XII and the Portuguese government on May 7, 1940. This document was followed by another Accordi Missionari by which both parties agreed to cooperate in the administration of the colonies. Article 24 of the Acto Colonial in referring to Portuguese colonies in Africa, states that the missions will be considered "an instrument of national civilization and colonial influence."[63] Through the patronado, a system of clerical privileges agreed upon in the Concordats, the Portuguese government paid the salaries of the bishop and priest, and also subsidized Catholic institutions. Since the concordats had standing in international law, and could not easily be terminated by the Vatican, they hindered the church from exercising positive influence in support of African nationalism in the former Portuguese colonies in southern Africa.[64]

While the global Catholic church was rendered impotent by the "historical baggage" it carried, the local churches (ecclesiola in ecclesia) could not do better for two interrelated reasons. First, since the Vatican has traditionally viewed foreign policy as its special preserve,[65] it has often acted as a "check" on the views of the local churches, especially if they were perceived to be "too progressive" and contrary to the church's global interest.[66] Second, since official church policy forbids local Catholic churches from commenting on issues affecting their sister churches without the latter's consent, progressive local Catholic churches have often been prevented from speaking out on crucial foreign policy issues. Consequently, the Catholic church, an institution that has historically enjoyed immense power in international relations has, until more recent times, tended to be more inclined, like the U.S., to a status quo position on the distribution of power.

Thus, in southern Africa, it was not the American Catholic hierarchy that confronted European colonialism and apartheid in southern Africa in the 1940s and 1950s. Rather, it was a small but vocal minority group of clergy and laity, who alerted the U.S. to its responsibilities in Africa. Founded in April 1927,[67] the Catholic Association for International Peace (CAIP), was perhaps the first major American Catholic group to call for the intervention of the U.S. government on behalf of human rights in South Africa and throughout the continent:

> The recent contest between the delegation of India and of South Africa in the General Assembly of the United Nations involving a matter of human rights has aroused an uneasy consciousness in the rest of the world that it cannot be wholly indifferent to the internal problems of

the African continent... the day has passed when the foreign policy of
the United States can consider itself absolved of all responsibility for
conditions which affect the lives of the millions of Africa's native
inhabitants.[68]

It compared the struggle of Africans for self-determination to the
American revolutionary war,[69] and tied America's interest in Africa to
the presence of millions of African-Americans in the U.S. who
consider the continent as their ancestral homeland.

Our position as the most powerful nation in the world demands that
part of our responsibility is to attend to the grievances of under
privileged races and peoples, particularly Africa to which thirteen
million of our citizens are bound by ties of racial solidarity...[70]

Finally, the CAIP sought to justify the African struggle in terms of
the church's just war theory:

The church teaches that one of the just causes of war is the securing of
the independence of a nation or the recovery of territory taken unjustly
from a people. Our war of independence was justified. But Africans
do not want war. They want, by constitutional means, to recover long-
lost territory and freedom. Our sympathies should be and are with
them.[71]

Generally, American church groups opposed to U.S. policy toward
southern Africa in the 1940s and 1950s adopted a policy of absolute
non-violent change to the problems of the region. Their overall impact
on U.S. policy was negligible.

However, after the Sharpeville massacre of 1960, some American
Protestant churches changed their tactics from non-violence to the
support of African armed struggle.[72] This placed them in direct
confrontation with U.S. policy, which advocated peaceful evolutionary
change as opposed to radical violent change. Direct action tactics,
such as mass marches and campaigns, were the tactics used to support
liberation in Africa.

In the 1960s, both Catholic and Protestant church groups
condemned the unilateral declaration of independence in Rhodesia
(1965) and Portuguese denial of human rights in its African territories.
The CAIP called Ian Smith's rebellion "a clear effort to preserve the
special privileges of the white minority and to protect the rights of its
African people. This display of racism, disguised as a freedom

movement, does a disservice to democratic government everywhere..."[73]

It joined the National Council of Churches (NCC) in expressing horror at Rhodesia's defiance and called on the U.S. government to assist in ending this "dangerous experiment in contemporary racism."[74]

In March 1967, the CAIP condemned racial discrimination in southern Africa as "an affront to human dignity and a menace to world peace."[75] It condemned Portuguese policy in Angola and Mozambique as racist and against human rights and urged "every American to end all forms of collaboration by the U.S. government and by private American organizations and individuals which give aid and comfort to injustice and evil throughout southern Africa."[76] On South Africa, it reaffirmed its opposition to apartheid and urged the U.S. government and its citizens to withhold financial and political support from the nationalist government.

Unfortunately, the progressive views of the CAIP on Africa did not represent those of the American Catholic bishops, the "authoritative teachers" within the U.S. Roman Catholic church. Until 1971, when they condemned American involvement in Vietnam,[77] U.S. Catholic bishops have traditionally supported the government on foreign policy issues. U.S. Africa policy was no exception.

Given their generally conservative role in the anti-colonial struggle, some writers have demanded that the churches must publicly disown colonialism if they are to regain any measure of respectability.[78] Bishop de Vries has reiterated the need for the churches to acknowledge and repent their collusion with colonialism in Africa.[79] Others have called not only for "prophetic repentance" from the churches, but also for an acknowledgment of the total lack of understanding they have shown over colonialism.[80]

In more recent times, however, the Catholic church hierarchy has shown some change of heart in its commitment to the anti-colonial struggle. For example, three recent actions of the Pope point to this change of attitude. First, in an address to African intellectuals in Yaounde, Cameroon, August 13 1985, John Paul II became the first major European leader to ask for Africa's forgiveness for the slave trade.[81] Second, in another address to Cameroonian leaders on August 12, 1985, he made a stinging condemnation of the apartheid system.

It is deplorable to see that a system of apartheid is still being prolonged. Through harsh repression it continues to create too many victims and tramples upon an elementary human right.[82]

Third, on February 10, 1989, the Vatican released its first document to deal solely with racism, a concept it defined as "contempt for a race characterized by its ethnic origin, color or language."[83] This important document also states that racial prejudice is an awareness of the biologically determined superiority of one man's race or ethnic group with respect to others, developed above all from the practice of colonization and slavery at the dawn of the modern era."[84] It observes that the

most obvious form of racism, in the strictest sense of the word to be found today is institutionalized racism. This type is still sanctioned by the constitution and laws of a country. It is justified by an ideology of the superiority of person from European stock over those of African or Indian origins or "colored, which is, by some, supported by an erroneous interpretation of the bible. This is the regime of apartheid or of separate development. This regime in the Republic of South Africa has long been characterized by a radical segregation in vast areas of public life, between the black, colored, Indian and white people, with only the latter, although numerically a minority, holding political power and considering themselves masters of by far the greatest part of the country ...South Africa is an extreme case of a vision of racial inequality.[85]

The 1970s and mid 1980s marked a period of increased efforts by American churches to change positively the direction of U.S. policy on southern Africa. These efforts became more militant in September 1970, when the WCC set aside $200,000 for nineteen liberation movements.[86] The Fund to Combat Racism, which was meant as humanitarian assistance to "movements that align themselves with the victims of racial injustice," gave half of its funds to southern Africa liberation movements.[87] The action of the WCC marked a point of departure in the attitude of the churches toward the anti-colonial struggle in Africa. Hitherto, the churches were solely engaged in the more traditional task of quietly educating, evangelizing and assisting refugee-victims of the independence struggle in southern Africa.[88]

However, in the U.S., the NCC paid only lip service to the fund and gave it little financial support. Worse still, with the exception of the United Methodist Church, most African American churches, which have hitherto played a crucial role in setting up the fund, gave it no financial support.[89] On the other hand, the United Church of Christ (UCC), a predominantly white church spent over $300,000 in aid to the liberation movements in 1973.[90] In setting up the fund to combat racism, however, the WCC asked that a distinction be made between "the morality of contributions to the defense and aid fund and soliciting arms for the guerrillas."[91]

It was, however, a distinction the Catholic church was not prepared to make--at least publicly. As usual, it preferred to work "quietly" among the refugee-victims of the anti-colonial struggle in southern Africa. Through ecumenical channels, it did render invaluable humanitarian assistance in the struggle for the liberation of southern Africa.[92] But the church was unprepared to support African recourse to armed resistance in the liberation struggle, a clear evidence of an inability to apply its just war theory in a real life situation. Rather, it advocated the policy of festina lente (hasten slowly), in the decolonization process, a position not substantially different from traditional U.S. Africa policy-support for peaceful and incremental change as opposed to radical or revolutionary change. The traditionally conservative position of the Vatican on the use of armed struggle in southern Africa may have been a product not only of its pacifist inclinations but also of its aversion to communism[93] and the protection of the church's global interest. It may also come from the caution and prudence of an organization which has lasted almost two millennia both by "divine providence" and by the ability to maneuver and secure its survival. Some critics of the catholic church's position have charged it of being more interested in feeding rather than freeing Africans from the clutches of colonialism.

Most U.S. media condemned the WCC for setting up the fund to combat racism. In a series of articles, The Readers Digest opposed the church organization, charging that it "had been taken over by communists."[94] Only the Christian Century supported the establishment of the fund, stating that the "church's long record of acquiescence in violence by the white establishments"[95] made it imperative.

The 1970s also saw the emergence of the Interfaith Center for Corporate Responsibility (ICCR), an interdenominational organ founded to influence U.S. policy by emphasizing the corporate responsibility of American corporations on South Africa. The United Methodist church was the first American church to take concrete action against South Africa by withdrawing its $10 million from the First National City bank because it aided Pretoria.[96]   Among higher education institutions, Hampshire College in Hadley, Massachusetts, became in 1976 the first U.S. college to use the weapon of divestment in the anti-apartheid struggle.[97]

The election of Carter in 1976 by a liberal bloc, including church groups and African Americans, the Soweto massacre a few months later, and the incorporation in July 1977 of Trans-Africa[98] led to increased demands for the use of American influence to support the anti-colonial struggle in southern Africa.   However, the overall influence of American church groups in the formulation of U.S. policy toward the region during the Carter administration is inconclusive.

The election of Reagan in 1980 brought about a conservative redirection of American policy toward southern African. Known as "constructive engagement," this policy and the support it received from fundamentalist protestant denominations led to a counterattack by the more liberal mainline church lobbies.[99] Generally, most liberal catholic and protestant groups have cooperated with other anti-apartheid groups in their opposition to the retrogressive policy of the Reagan administration toward southern Africa. However, even though they have participated in anti-apartheid demonstrations and congressional efforts, the actual influence of the churches on U.S. policy toward the region during the Reagan administration is also inconclusive. This dissertation will examine American church influence on U.S. southern Africa during both the Carter and Reagan administrations.

An examination of U.S. church group influence on U.S. southern Africa policy is necessary given the sheer moral and humanitarian force engendered by the problems of the region and the expectation that American churches, the "custodians of the nation's conscience," should have played a more significant role in the shaping of U.S. policy. This has apparently not happened for both organizational and systemic reasons. Schattschneider has indicted interest groups for performing poorly as "mobilizers of the interests of large numbers of people".[100] Both Dahl and Walker address the crisis of American democracy in the context of elite predominance of its political and institutional arrangements, that has rendered it inadequate to deal with both domestic and international problems. Dahl contends that America's commitment to an international role as a world power has robbed it of its democratic traditions.[101] Walker observes that since American democracy has been stripped of its "radical elan" and is left with only a "diluted utopian vision," it has been rendered an inadequate guide to the stormy realities of the twentieth century.[102] In southern Africa, the traditional dominance of elite business, military-strategic and government bureaucratic interests in the shaping of U.S. policy, has led to a myopic rather than a hypertrophic view of the realities of the region. This dominance was perpetuated by the unwillingness of the churches to make politicians see religion as a force to be reckoned with through a congregation that is organized, informed and energized on issues important to them. "Official reports, convention resolution, public statements have little effect. Only an aroused public opinion will have any effect on those who make and execute policy."[103]

The purpose of this study is to investigate and analyze the influence of Catholic and Protest groups as on U.S. southern Africa policy as it relates to the repeal of the Clark Amendment, the importation of Rhodesian chrome, and the enactment of the 1986 Anti- Apartheid Act.

HYPTHOSES

This study will test the following hypotheses:

1. U.S. southern Africa policy significantly reflects the interest foreign policy preferences of American religious groups.

2. Groups are more likely to influence decisions made by "social processes" than those by "intellective processes."

3. The ability of groups to influence foreign policy depends on their resources and other factors.

The hypotheses are drawn from the research findings and theoretical views of interest group influence on foreign policy espoused by Lester W. Milbrath. Basically, Milbrath sees interest group influence as "a communication process between citizens and governments as they make foreign policy decisions". According to him, foreign policy decisions are made through "social" and "intellective" processes. By "social processes," Milbrath identifies those foreign policy issues which share similar characteristics and are, therefore, amenable to group influence. For example, these issues are shared by both the president and congress, involve direct, visible rewards and punishments to different segments of the society, and last for a longer time than non-crisis events. They also afford more points of access and opportunities to interest groups and stimulate more lobbying activities. By "intellective processes," Milbrath identifies those issues that are primarily decided by rational calculation. They also have a short life span and are crisis-oriented. The decisions based normally on these issues are made by a small and closed group of people, with little outside input. In "intellective process" issues, the president's predominance is almost total vis-a-vis the congress.

However, it should be noted that although the three decisions in this study were made by "social processes," there was still some intellectual input.

Milbrath also ties group influence to its resource base, which includes the ability to identify the major actors involved in the decision-making process, the capability to have access to decision-makers, and the strength to make sure its message reaches policy makers. It is, however, important to emphasize that all these activities will be impossible if the group has no money, "the oxygen of politics".

The application of Milbrath's theories to the study of the influence of American religious groups on foreign policy is justifiable for two interrelated reasons. First, even though he virtually ignores religious groups in his study, his emphasis on the communications process as an ideal method of studying group influence on foreign policy applies also to church groups. Second, Milbrath's theories will, therefore, be useful tools in the study of the traditional influence--peddling tactics used by church groups, namely congressional hearings, grass-roots mobilization and research. This approach will also help in the study of the communications processes within religious interest groups as well as their linkages with foreign policy decision-makers. A more indepth explanation of Milbrath's theory of group influence on foreign policy will be given in the theoretical framework.

CHAPTER II - Theoretical Framework

Ever since the birth of the American experiment in republican democracy, the role and influence of interest groups in the American political process has been a source of fascination and controversy among scholars, politicians, and analysts. In the Federalist papers, Madison ascribed to "factions" or interest groups a negative but necessary role within the American political process. Defining interest groups as a "group of individuals who are united and actuated by some common impulse or passion, or of interest, adverse to the rights of other citizens, or to the permanent and aggregate interests of the community,"[104] he sees the regulation of conflicting group interests as the "principal task of modern legislation and involves the spirit of party and faction in the necessary and ordinary operations of government.[105]

With the emergence of group theory in the 1950s and 1960s as a predominant focus of scholarly attention, especially among political scientists, scholars like Bentley, Latham, Truman and others have hypothesized both positive and negative roles for interest groups. They act as "connections" between the people and the more formalized institutions of government,[106] as "links" that connect the citizen and government,[107] recruiters of elites, agents or inhibitors of societal change, political socializers, and molders of public opinion.[108] Groups also transform individual needs and aspirations into societal norms, and economic power into social power into political decisions.[109] As groups, churches maintain political stability by "either service to the existing order by urging devotion to it, or service to it by helping its victims to find consolation in the visions of another world."[110] Not even the state is left out as an important participant in the governmental process. Bentley introduced the scientific definition of the state as an interest that could be conceived "as an interest group itself."[111]

The negative role of groups has been articulated by scholars like Lowi, Parenti, and Stern. In their view, groups atrophy institutions of popular control, maintain old and create new structures of privilege, and are basically conservative.[112] Even pluralism, the traditional model used by scholars to explain group process in a democracy have either been totally rejected as unrealistic,[113] or have been branded "pluralism for a few."[114] The critical dangers posed by some American groups to the health of the American political process have also been identified.[115]

In foreign policy per se, the relationship between American interest groups and U.S. foreign policy is no less controversial and inconclusive. Nonetheless, ever since the publication of the Snyder framework,[116] scholars have been able to reduce foreign policy behavior to five principal categories: systematic, environment, societal, governmental, and idiosyncratic or psychological.[117]

Several scholars of the societal school, like Dahl and Almond, who see foreign policy behavior of a state as the external manifestation of domestic societal forces, or from "national character," a national "model personality," or from the "political culture," have explained U.S. foreign policy in the context of the influence of American domestic interest groups on American policy.

In his book, Congress and Foreign Policy: It's Organization and Control, Dahl sees the problems of American foreign policy as emanating from the nature of the American society, from the "enormous increase in the impact of foreign policies on the preferences of many groups and the fact that decisions of foreign policy take place in the social and political milieu of mass democracy."[118] According to him, mass democracy has two implications for U.S. foreign policy.

1) It caters to an extraordinarily broad range of groups and strata that insist that their claims and interests be considered in the making of foreign policy; and

2) It forces policy makers to take into consideration the possible effect of policy decisions on virtually every strata of society.

Dahl states that groups that hold intensive views on foreign policy and act upon them have an important influence on foreign policy, and that their intensity tends to outweigh the influence of larger groups that fail to act on their views. For example, he claims that ethnic and religious minorities are often more influential than a "passive majority." Among the religious groups, he claims that Catholics influence American foreign policy "out of all proportion to its size," because:

1) Many of its members hold their views with intensity, i.e., their views determine their political conduct.

2) They are strategically located within the political system.[119]

However, Dahl warns against the equation of interest activity with influence. Attempts should be made, he asserts, 'to test propositions about indirect influence and vertical relations on policy of group participation in the larger political process of opinion formation.' But, the author makes his assumptions of Catholics without any systematic and comparative analysis of the group in relation to U.S. foreign policy.

For Almond, the attitudes and opinions of Americans should not be understood merely as responses to objective problems and situations, but as conditioned by culturally imposed qualities of character, which he summarized as tending to be "automistic rather than corporate, worldly rather than unworldly, highly mobile rather than traditional, compulsive rather than relaxed, and externally directed rather than autonomous."[120]

Almond discusses the shortcomings of both scholars and elites as participants in the foreign policy debate. Scholars of public opinion and foreign policy, he observes, fall into the democratic error of "minimizing the inherent social and political stratification of influence of American politics." They fail to differentiate analytically between the impact on foreign policy of a traditionally apathetic "general public" and a generally knowledgeable and active "attentive public," whom he calls the "influential." This typology of foreign policy elites or the influential is made up of "political elites," "bureaucratic elites," "interest elites," and "communications elites." Of all these groups, he identifies the most effective opinion leaders as the "vast number of vocational, community, and institutional "notables," known and trusted men and women--clergymen and influential lay churchmen and women, teachers and the like--with a personal following."

Almond argues that if elite performance in foreign policy is based on "democratic discipline, ideological consensus, or the development of a systematic and integrative mentality, two primary 'training elites'-- teachers and clergymen--are important." But both professionals, according to the author, fall short because they tend to be "bearers of moral and political idealism...are susceptible to millennial hopes, and thereby lay the groundwork for cynical rejections and disillusionments among their charges." He further accuses them of a "moral dualism" that is responsible for the instability in American opinion: "They set up aspiration which cannot be fulfilled, and inculcate principles of conduct which cannot be effective.[121] Furthermore, Almond indicts teachers and clergy of an inability to deal   with real problems of military and political security. They have

> a penchant for escapism, which often lies at the basis of their choice of these professions (and) is encouraged by a curricula badly adapted to broad character-molding and ideal-setting function these elites are called on to perform.[122]

However, in spite of their leaders' shortcomings, most U.S. church organizations, the author asserts, "adhere to the foreign policy consensus...and have consistently supported most of the foreign policy steps taken since the end of the war." The author does not identify the reason(s) for the attitudinal difference between church leadership and church membership on foreign policy issues.

Using the communications process, other scholars, like Cohen and Milbrath, have sought to analyze the influence relationship between interest groups and the foreign policy-making process. In his book, The Influence of Non-Governmental Groups on Foreign Policy, Cohen states that the absence of empirical research in group dynamics has led to a "legend" of pressure group influence in foreign policy.[123] In order to avoid such assumptions about interest groups, Cohen's principal aim is to find out what "non-governmental groups or individuals have major effects on the making and execution of foreign policy." Such an enterprise, he observes, is difficult, given the variety of interest groups involved in a policy, and the need to differentiate between "mere support" and "major support." The problem of identifying influence may even be exacerbated by the fact that some interest groups may even have significant influence by their "silence,"[124] that is, when such silence means a preference for a status quo policy position.

According to Cohen, most interest groups in foreign policy like to influence public opinion, and by so doing change the political climate and may exert some influence on foreign policy. Their success, however, depends on a variety of factors: the issue they are trying to influence must not be in the "public eye," it must deal with a very narrow subject matter or with technical instead of political issues; and it is submerged in more dramatic or compelling issues of foreign or domestic policy so that the "attentive public" is so small that interest groups can easily stake the legitimacy of their interests.[125] All the same, the author opines that the influence of interest groups on foreign policy issues is limited to the "area of their special policy interest."

For groups to have maximum influence on policy, Cohen observes that two critical factors must be noted. (1) They must have access to congressmen and be able to issue electoral threats, especially "when the interest groups involved are organizationally and numerically from important elements in political strategic constituencies." (2) There must be an "ideological connection" between the "would-be-influential" and the policy makers since the latter tend to lend their support to groups with whom they share ideological or political affinity.

Cohen, however, reiterates that while these two groups are influential on certain occasions, all groups, even the reputedly most powerful, often fail in their attempts to influence policy. Nowhere is this failure more obvious, he asserts, than in "large national organizations commonly placed in the categories of civic, professional, fraternal, women, ideological, and even religious groups," which he claims, fail most of the time as they attempt to influence foreign policy. Certain groups lack influence because of "institutional or situational" factors. Moreover, for real influence to exist, a group's interest must be "recognized as legitimate by policy-makers with whom they must share a "congruence of opinion and sentiment." Equally important to group influence is the "consonance of the policy being advocated by a group with the prevailing political temper of the times," i.e., the political atmosphere must be conducive to interest group pressures.

In his study, "Interest Groups and Foreign Policy," Milbrath seeks to find out the process by which interest groups influence foreign policy, which groups are likely to have influence on which issues, how to classify groups vis-a-vis their posture toward foreign policy, and whether groups act differently when trying to influence foreign policy decisions than they do when trying to influence domestic policy decisions.[126]

Basically, he sees interest group influence as "a communication process between citizens and governments as they make foreign policy decisions." He states that before any influence can occur, the "influencee" must receive and consider a message from the "influencer." But, whereas all transmissions of influence constitute some form of message, he claims, "not all communications transmit influence, some transmit only information."

Milbrath also insists that decisions on foreign policy that involve direct, visible (usually economic) rewards and/or punishments to different sections of the society tend to be shared by the president and congress. They also tend to be social rather than "intellectual" in process and to stimulate more lobbying by groups at various points of access. According to him, groups desiring to influence policy must meet three conditions for success. First, the group should be able to identify the major actors involved in the decisions and the various stages through which their deliberations must pass. Second, the group must have access to the decision-makers. Third, the group must make sure its message gets to the targeted policy makers. Thus, the group must make sure its message penetrates the "perceptual screen" of the decision-makers by passing the "legitimacy and credibility tests." A decision-maker considers a message legitimate if he believes that the interest group has a right to lobby him on the issue. He considers a message credible if the relevant interest group has a reputation for honesty and accuracy. A message may also attain credibility by the sheer force of the idea or argument it contains.

In conclusion, Milbrath suggests twelve hypotheses on interest group influence on foreign policy; <u>inter alia</u>, they are:

1. The possibility for interest group influence on foreign policy varies with the issue.
2. Groups are more likely to influence decisions made by "social processes" than those made by "intellective processes."
3. Foreign policy decisions that deal with direct visible (economic) rewards and/or punishments involving different parts of the society tend to be shared by Congress and the President, are social rather than intellectual in process, and are amenable to interest group activity.
4. Issues that attract the attention of "special publics," but little general public attention, are more open to group influence than issues that attract wide and/or intense public interest.
5. An increase in the importance of a decision or in the level of crisis, attracts more groups seeking to exert influence.
6. Group influence on an issue tends to be higher, the less important that issue.
7. The longer a decision is allowed to gestate, the more open it is to group influence.
8. The ability of interest groups to influence public opinion on foreign policy is severely limited.

The author virtually ignores ethnic and religious interest groups in his analysis of group behavior and foreign policy. He claims that non-economic foreign policy interest groups, which are usually small and underfinanced, tend to emphasize broad issues of war and peace. Overall, he insists that group influence on foreign policy is slight now and will be in the future.

The relative political influence of voluntary associations on both members and non-members has been investigated by scholars and analysts. In their study, "Differential Political Influence of Voluntary Associations," Freeman and Showel measured the influence of groups on the readiness of both members and non-members to follow the groups' political advice on domestic and foreign policy issues.[127] According to the authors, while the influence of associations on policy is usually based on their own assumptions, the effectiveness of groups to influence the electorate varies considerably. Some groups exert "positive influence" i.e., they influence the electorate, made up of members and/or non-members who follow the path advocated by the group. They can also exert "negative influence" i.e., they influence the electorate made up of members and/or non-members to follow a path not advocated by the group.

The authors discovered that while veterans, business, and political groups exert positive influence beyond the confines of their membership, the Catholic church has significant influence among its membership.

In conclusion, Freeman and Showel propose the following hypotheses: (1) Groups may vary as to the extent of their net political influence. (2) Groups do not vary widely in their ability to exercise positive influence over their membership in the political sphere. (3) Groups vary widely in their ability to positively influence members and non-members. Business, political, and veteran groups exert the widest positive influence; labor and church groups, the narrowest positive influence. (4) The most influential groups are not necessarily those which have the specific objective of influencing the electorate. (5) The only relationship between net influence and size that seems relevant is that between size and rank on the membership net influence continuum.

It was not until 1974 that Ogene linked the group phenomena to U.S. foreign policy making process on Africa. In his seminal work, Interest Groups and the Shaping of Foreign Policy, he attempts to identify the groups interested in Africa, their interests and foreign policy preference, lobbying tactics, level of influence on U.S. policy on African issues, and factors that determine that influence.[128]

He identifies six ways by which groups exert influence on U.S. policy toward Africa: (1) By affecting developments within African societies, groups affect the external environment of U.S. foreign policy and thereby place some constraints on that policy; (2) by acting as a direct and credible source of information for policy makers, or by articulating interest in African problems, groups influence policy; (3) through the conscious or unconscious transformation of group interests into the interests and goals of governmental decision-making units, groups influence policy; (4) by supporting or opposing alternative policies, groups influence policy; (5) by facilitating or obstructing the implementation of decisions already made, groups exert influence on policy; and (6) by promoting or modifying the intended effect of a decision, groups affect the subsequent feedback information and policy review.[129] A group's influence is considered significant if it takes any of the six forms.

Finally, Ogene offers the following hypotheses on the determinants of group influence on foreign policy.

1. The most important factor in group influence on policy is the "control and use of such resources as funds, prestige, and lobbying skills." The conventionality and the group's interest in an African issue also contribute to its influence.

2. The desire and will to exert influence were important. However, policy makers could consider a group's interest without its effort to exert influence.[130]

3. The availability of channels and a group's efficient use of them to decision-makers are important determinants of group influence. Interest group links among government groups are very important.[131]

4. While groups with interest in "tangible" resources are more influential than those with interest in "symbolic" resources, these who have interest in both have the greatest influence on foreign policy.

Other scholars have analyzed the impact of environmental factors on the foreign behavior of states. In their study "Environmental Factors in the Study of International Politics," the Sprouts state that in the study of foreign policy behavior of states, a clear distinction should be drawn "between political attitudes and policy decisions, on the one hand, and, on the other hand, the layouts in space or other states of affairs which we shall call operational results of decisions."[132] According to them, it is only when environmental factors are "related to the attitudes and decisions which comprise a states" foreign policy, that they are considered in a policy-making process. Thus, what matters in policy making, the authors attest, is "how the policy maker imagines the milieu to be, not how it actually is."

The Sprouts assert that the higher position officials occupy in government, the more remote they are from the "operational environment in which their decisions are executed." For, on most issues, individuals and groups responsible for decisions often depend on materials prepared at the lower levels of the organization. Moreover, while in a "man-milieu" relationship, policy-making is viewed as a "deliberative process that is carried out in an intellectual environment of rationality and logic", policy decisions "may reflect not only defective environmental knowledge but also illogical reasoning as well."

In conclusion, the Sprouts state that: (1) Ecological viewpoint and framework is a useful approach to foreign policy analysis, and (2) it is important to distinguish the relationship of environmental factors to policy decisions, and to the operational results. For in policy-making and the content of policy decisions, what matters is how the policymaker imagines the milieu to be, not what it actually is in operational results of decisions, what matters is "how things really are, not what the policy-maker imagines them to be."

LITERATURE REVIEW

Since it encompasses the last remnants of colonialism and white minority rule, few regions of the world have attracted the attention of scholars and analysts as much as southern Africa. Studies of U.S. policy toward southern Africa as well as the rest of the continent have been characterized by three important factors: the overemphasis of the role of "systematic and aggregate factors" and the neglect of American domestic groups, especially religious interest groups; the low profile ascribed to southern Africa in the hierarchy of U.S. global interests; and the traditional inconsistency that has plagued U.S. policy. These views of southern Africa and the U.S. response to them have been expressed in books, journals, and other learned publications.

Vernon McKay's "Southern Africa and Its Implications for American Policy" offers a good background study of U.S. policy toward southern Africa. According to him, the problems of southern Africa were those of white minority regimes in Rhodesia, South Africa and Portuguese colonialism in Angola and Mozambique.[133] While agreeing that the political and social evolution of these countries followed different paths, they were, nonetheless, attempts to "maintain varying forms of white supremacy."

McKay states that the U.S. had only minor strategic and economic interests in southern Africa, while its greatest interest is clearly a political interest in fostering the right kind of balance, freedom and stability. However, this political interest, he asserts, was threatened by the racial policies of the white colonial and minority regimes in the region, since it acted as a continuing stimulant to the Soviet Union and China to renew their efforts, and were therefore an irritant to peaceful coexistence between the great powers.

Finally, McKay claims that the U.S. has traditionally supported the quest for freedom in southern Africa by condemning white minority and colonial regimes in the region, but its condemnation has had "little effect." Other than mere condemnation, the author does not really identify the ways and means to make U.S. policy more effective. He does not identify any American interest groups that could have helped to change U.S. policy.

A more conservative but important book on U.S. southern African relations is L.S. Gann and Peter Duignan's book Why South Africa Will Survive.[134] The importance of this book lies not merely on its facile explanation of U.S. strategic and economic interests in southern Africa and its implications for American global strategy, but on its fairly indepth and extensive analysis of pro and anti-South African interest groups in the United States.

According to the authors, the problem of South Africa is of concern only to a minority of Americans because it is far too remote. Since South Africa has no ethnic lobby in the U.S. and receives only vague sympathy from "Middle America," Gann and Duignan predict that such sympathy will only become a force in America if racial hostilities within the United States were to be violently exacerbated.

The authors identify some American corporations with interest in South Africa as sympathetic to Pretoria, but not as powerful as liberals claim. They state that the closest thing to a South African lobby in the U.S. are conservative groups such as the gun lobby, former Green Berets, and Evangelical Christians.

The anti-South African interest groups in the U.S. are 'radical organizations,' unions, black Americans, the liberal media, the establishment churches, academic and the Afrophile segment of the federal bureaucracy. They call African-Americans the weakest of the anti-South African lobbies because "they have not, until now, been able to mobilize their strength to anything like its full potential." African-Americans, the authors assert, are unable to rally over South Africa because they "have no real religious, linguistic or cultural links with Africa." Moreover, "to help the revolution abroad," they declare, "black Americans first have to join the establishment at home." They ascribe the limited influence of TransAfrica to black destiny which is that of an underpriviledge group in the U.S.

According to the authors, academic and clerical organizations have more influence on U.S. southern Africa policy than blacks. He identifies churches with a special stake in South Africa as the World Council of Churches (WCC) and its American affiliate, the National Council of Churches (NCC). They label both of them as "leftist-oriented" groups whose influence is exaggerated. Both writers opine that the churches, who still interpret southern African issues in missionary terms, can only become influential if "they find powerful allies within the ranks of the legislature and the' bureaucracy."

They credit changing public opinion against South Africa in the U.S. to the liberal media, a "reserve army" for progressive causes--and to the "knowledge elite," a new class of academically educated and upper middle class engaged in such professions as healing, teaching and scientific research.

But in spite of a fairly broad analysis of American groups interested in U.S. policy toward South Africa, Gann and Duignan fail to identify systematically, analyze and compare the interrelationships between the various interest groups and their impact on U.S. policy.

Some scholars have analyzed the role and influence exercised by African Americans on U.S. policy toward Africa as a whole and on southern Africa in particular. In his study, "The Influence of Black Americans on U.S. Foreign Policy Toward Africa," Challenor identifies three main reasons why "racial hyphenates," unlike "ethnic hyphenates," have had insignificant influence on policy toward their ancestral lands:

> the absence of black political power historically as a result of
> disenfranchisement in the South and the neutralization of the   black
> vote in the North through gerrymandering and other means as well as
> the later predictability of the black electorate; the factor of low esteem
> accorded to blacks and to Africa; and official attempts to discourage
> close effective links between Africans and African Americans.[135]

Nonetheless, the author states that even though historically, African American concern with Africa has been characterized by escalating periods of maximum and minor interest, it currently competes with four other strategic options: "integration, internal statism or black nationalism, culture nationalism, and emigrationism."[136]

First, Challenor examines the "little-publicized black attempts to influence economic and political developments in Africa" from the post-Civil War era to toward the end of the Second World War, and concludes that due to the "political impotence of Afro Americans," African American missionaries had a more positive impact on Africa than "black political brokers who tried to modify U.S. policy."[137] Black political impotence, according to her, is the product of certain deficiencies of American domestic politics as well as cleavages within the African-American community. On the one hand, disenfranchisement of most Southern blacks coupled with the hostile attitudes of U.S. officials toward black nations undermined black influence. On the other hand, the strategic disagreement between proponents of "submission, internal statism/separation, emigrationism, assimilation, and cultural nationalism," hemorrhaged black power. This was a period when intellectuals and clergymen played a dominant role within the black community.

Second, the author analyzes the new black American interest in Africa, which is both a product of the civil rights movement and African independence, and argues that certain factors will make this interest more permanent. First, since almost all African countries have become independent and now control both their resources as well as their global relations, black American interests in Africa is more focused on southern Africa. Second, black electoral power has the potential to influence the political process. Third, improved communication, higher academic levels, and the increase of black studies programs, has promoted renewed interest in Africa. Fourth, the increasing concern of the middle class in African affairs has strengthened overall black interest in Africa. Fifth, there is wider overall contact between Africans and African Americans. And finally, the recrudescence of black American interest in Africa comes at a time when blacks have greater access to equal opportunities, but nonetheless, reject many American values. One would have thought the reverse to be the case.

Challenor also documents some of the roles played by both individuals and various black groups in their attempt to influence U.S. Africa policy. Among these were Ghana's independence and the development of close relations between Nkrumah and DuBois, the efforts of Malcolm X, Hatcher, and Diggs, and of groups like the American Negro Leadership Conference on Africa (ANCLA), the Congress of African Peoples (CAP), and the African Heritage Association.

But it was the formation of TransAfrica that, according to the author, has had the "most remarkable impact on opinions and decision-making on African and Caribbean issues." Some of its early successes included the successful lobbying of the U.S. government to retain sanctions against the Smith regime in Rhodesia and alerting the Organization of African Unity (OAU) that Congress might lift Rhodesian sanctions following Smith's announcement of the internal settlement in Rhodesia.

Finally, Challenor identifies several constraints on an organized black lobby for Africa: "the prevailing mood of American diplomacy, the force of black domestic interests, black political culture, disunity among the black leadership class, and official discouragement." According to her, "events suggest that the persistence of racism in the United States will prevent the majority society from according the same tolerance to blacks seeking to influence their ancestral land that has been afforded to other ethnic hyphenate groups engaged in such activities."[138]

Walters does not share Challenor's pessimism about the "political impotence of Afro-Americans" on U.S. policy toward Africa. He assesses the linkage between the U.S. and Africa, the policy interests of African Americans, and uses the quest for South African independence as a way to explain black attempts to "develop systematic influence relationships."[139]

Walters identifies two basic problems of the African American attempt to influence U.S. Africa policy. One is the multiplicity of African nations, a problem that leads him to state that "there is no such thing as the relationship between the United States and 'Africa' except in the most thematic sense of the way in which it relates to each nation on the continent of Africa." The other is the legitimacy of black interests in Africa.

In spite of these problems, however, he insists that blacks are not only interested in Africa, but are also "involved in both domestic and international policy formation processes from the base of a more mobile and influential society." He traces the efforts of black leaders and organizations, who since 1960, have attempted to influence U.S. Africa policy on two important issues: lingering colonialism and development. They include such black leaders as Diggs and Hatcher, and organizations like the National Black Leadership Conference on Africa and TransAfrica. The author credits TransAfrica with preventing the Smith-Muzorewa government from receiving the support of Washington, and thus, opening the way for Mugabe's election.

Walters states that the growing influence of TransAfrica is also evident in its struggle with Reagan's policy of constructive engagement toward South Africa. It was a struggle that led to the arrest of Robinson, Fauntroy, and Barry, and brought the "Free South Africa Movement" (FSAM) into existence. The grassroots protest engendered by the FSAM led to increased divestment in cities and colleges across the country, and ultimately to the passage of the Anti-Apartheid Act of 1985.

Unlike Lemelle, Challenor, and Barnett, who state that "an ethnic model of policy influence is inappropriate to an analysis of black influences," Walters reiterates the importance of "race subordination" as the central problem of the barriers to the exercise of influence." He also sees it as a "continuing and vital basis of policy education and mobilization," especially since the overarching political system within which blacks exist, determines the goals of the authoritative decision-makers, whose interests are averse to the foreign policy interests of the African American community.

In conclusion, Walters suggests that the linkage between the black presence in both the executive and legislative branches and other non-governmental organizations is the best strategy for the black community. Nonetheless, he further suggests that "mobilization external to institutions, is, on balance, more important in building both public opinion and political pressure for a policy agenda to be considered by policy making institutions."[140]

In their analysis of blacks and U.S. African policy, both Challenor and Walters gave only tangential treatment of a very important institution for mass mobilization especially within the African-American community and indeed, within American society--the church. And since the apartheid system is based on a pseudo econo-theological base, one would have thought that greater and more indepth analytical attention should have been given to the role(s) churches have played, and, still play, in the 'moral' crusade against apartheid.

In a very important book In Whose Interest, Kevin Danaher seeks to illuminate "the gulf between the rhetoric of policy--as preached and the reality of policy-as-practiced, to examine the ways in which U.S. policy has had an anti-democratic effect both at home and abroad: abroad, by sustaining white minority rule, and at home, by deceiving the American public".[141]

Emphasizing the impact of the U.S. position on the global economy and its implications for its South Africa policy, the author offers some explanations for American support for Pretoria. First, prior to the political independence of black Africa and the emergence of black power in America, some corporations and government agencies, like the Pentagon, CIA, and the Commerce Department, which were pro-Pretoria, constituted the "main constituencies for U.S. policy toward South Africa." There was no strong and well-organized anti-apartheid opposition in the country, American politicians and policy makers ignored the oppression of the black majority by the white minority in southern Africa. But as Africans and black Americans gained access to the world's political and economic institutions, Danaher says that in order to manage this change, U.S. policy makers developed a policy "straddle" in an attempt to placate both the anti-apartheid government and corporate groups interested in U.S. southern Africa policy.

However, the increased strengths of these opposing constituencies have made it more difficult for U.S. policy makers to reconcile American economic and strategic interests with humanitarian interests.

Danaher claims that in spite of substantial public support for tougher measures against South Africa, no U.S. administration "has ever tried a policy of real material pressure on the white minority." He identifies U.S. corporations in South Africa, which "wield extraordinary influence in Washington," as the stumbling block to tougher measures against Pretoria.

Finally, Danaher proposes strategies to counteract the influence of the wealthy and influential American corporations. One such measure is the education of Americans on the correlation between apartheid and bread-and-butter issues. For example, they should be told that American workers lose their jobs when corporations close their plants and move to South Africa in search of bigger profits. Another measure that needs to be emphasized is the building of coalitions between the anti-apartheid movement and groups like the anti-nuclear movement.

Danaher's analysis of American domestic groups is both narrow and tangential. The influence of American corporations on U.S. policy is overemphasized, while the importance and role of religious groups is underestimated. Moreover, there is no indepth and systematic analysis of the policy preferences and interactions of American domestic groups.

An obvious lacuna in the literature of U.S. southern African relations is the absence of studies of American religious groups and their impact on U.S. policy. Paul Deats' study, "U.S. Religious Institutions and South Africa",[142] a good attempt to describe and analyze the role and influence of American religious groups on U.S. policy, attempts to fill this gap.

According to the author, in spite of differences of opinion, a remarkable consensus for change in South Africa exists among church leaders. These differences include: the nature of change; the place of change; the perception of change; the real locus of influence for change; and the ability of churches to influence change. In spite of these differences, however, the author states that several factors make the role of leaders of churches strategic: strong institutional and personal ties exist between American and South African churches with large black and colored memberships, especially (but not exclusively) the Roman Catholic church; the possession by the churches of a 'latent moral sensitivity...that can be aroused and instructed by leaders of U.S.

and South African churches;' the impact of black preachers in predominantly black congregations; and the challenge which apartheid as a synthesis of white nationalism and neo-Calvinist theology poses for the churches.

Deats also discusses the question of corporate responsibility, the 'main' channel of church involvement. He credits such church groups as the Interfaith Center on Corporate Responsibility (ICCR) as leaders in the efforts to raise social consciousness in corporations in which they hold stock. He observes that more than any other church, it was the NCC that "has taken the initiative, setting the tone of and the stage for action by many other church bodies."

Nonetheless, Deats opines that while the churches exert a subtle influence on the ethos and general sensitivity of the nation, which can extend beyond their influence on specific decisions of governments and corporations, church leaders often "overestimate their potential on governmental decisions on issues of religious social concern."

Finally, the author predicts the expansion of dialogue between American churches and their black and white counterparts. This could lead the American churches to seek alternatives to the controversial WCC's program to combat racism special fund by providing direct funds to allied South African denominational churches. Moreover, increased church influence through corporate channels will lead to the exertion of more pressure on Congress and the president.

Deats' study is deficient in several ways. First, it presumes that American religious group response to southern Africa issues is tantamount to influence on those issues. Second, it is not a systematic, quantitative, or comparative analysis of U.S. policy. Third, the various interrelationships and interactions between the various groups and their impact on policy were neither described nor systematically analyzed.

This study will seek to correct some of the loopholes and inadequacies identified in the aforementioned research. An attempt will be made to present a more balanced and objective analysis of U.S. southern African policy.

METHODOLOGY AND PROBLEMS

This study will begin with a historical analysis of the evolution of American Catholic and protestant group interest in southern Africa, and the impact of that interest on subsequent U.S. policy. While it is not a replication of the Ogene study, already summarized in the literature review, it will, when necessary, coopt, adapt, and alter his methodological approach to its peculiar circumstances.

Three hypotheses of group influence will be tested by the use of three cases of U.S. southern African policy. These cases were not randomly selected since such a procedure could lead to the inclusion of issues that lack sufficient data. Rather, they were chosen for several reasons. First, the cases have enough data necessary for testing hypotheses. Second, they possess common characteristics that would make them generalizable and theoretically relevant. They belong to a typology of foreign policy cases. Third, the issues involved were shared by both the President and Congress. Fourth, the cases deal with the decolonization process in Africa, a policy area that is supposedly the "Achilles's heel" of church group interest on the continent.

Foreign policy decisions may also be divided according to the nature of decisions into three parts; crisis decisions; innovative decisions and routine decisions. Crisis decisions are those foreign policy decisions "characterized by high threats to a nation's vital interests, by short decision time, and by the element of surprise." Innovative decisions involve the "setting of new policy guidelines or the reviewing of existing ones." Routine decisions are those that have set-guidelines for implementing policy. The three cases to be studied are a combination of crisis and innovative decisions. It is the contention of this writer that crisis decisions need not have a short decision time. Southern Africa has been in a state of "perpetual crisis" ever since the arrival of European colonialism in the 15th century.

The study and comparison of the influence of American Catholic and protestant groups on U.S. southern Africa policy will follow this procedure:

1. The relevant interest groups, the description of their interests, and policy preferences will be identified. While such an identification will not show the degree of influence the groups have on the foreign policy cases chosen it will, at least, prove the existence of Catholic and Protestant group interest on southern Africa issues.
2. The direct and indirect relationships between each group and the decision-making process will be noted. These relationships will not show the actual influence of the groups on the decision-making process; they will, no doubt, establish real linkages between both.
3. The relevant activities of each group as it attempts to influence the decision-making process will be analyzed. This will be done by the identification of the main social processes by which Catholic and Protestant groups seek to influence, for example, through

congressional hearings, research, and mass-mobilization. When possible, the amount of money spent by the groups on their social action programs will be noted not only because it shows how important certain issues are to a group, money has also been found to give groups access to decision-makers. However, it may be impossible to identify the amount of money groups spent to lobby on thethree issues to be examined.

4. The final results taken by decision-makers (decisions outputs) will be described and compared to the interest and foreign policy preferences of the interest groups. In this way, the actual influence of the religious interest groups will be discovered.

The study of the influence of religious interest group on U.S. foreign policy poses several problems. The methodological problem includes the measurement of two levels of influence. One is the problem of determining "influence order," especially since many influence relations represent "closed hoop" systems (i.e., one in which variables within the system are so related that one can trace a chain of relationships from one variable to the other and back to the original starting point without retracing one's steps) either directly or through the operation of the so-called "rule of anticipated reactions." The other is the problem of the dimensionality of influence in which it is unclear how to rate the extent of influence. The problem of coalitional lobbying in the measurement of influence has been noted.[143]

For the purpose of this study, the exercise of influence will be defined as the ability to affect the "policies of others than self."[144]

Another problem posed by this study is constitutional, and arises out of the yet unresolved tensions between church and state in American politics. This tension, which arises out of the separation clause, prohibits the state from sponsoring a particular religion. It does not prohibit religious groups from participating in politics.

THE SETTING

The study will be arranged in the following order:

Chapter One: The Introduction

The chapter will address the general problem and objective of the study. The hypotheses will be introduced, the methodology for testing the hypotheses described, problems raised, and the sources of research data identified. The core of the methodological approach to this study is the analysis of the social processes by which religious interest groups seek to influence U.S. southern African policy. For example: Do religious groups significantly influence U.S. policy through appearances at congressional hearings, research, and mass-mobilization at the local diocesan and parish levels? Such an approach will help to arrive at conclusions on the hypotheses.

Chapter Two: Theoretical Framework

This chapter will identify and examine the interactions of interest groups involved in foreign policy formulation towards South Africa. Special attention will be paid to the tactics adopted by Catholic and protestant groups in their attempts to influence policy. Did they apply traditional church methods such as congressional hearings, grass-roots mobilization, et cetera? Did they spend a lot of money on this particular issue?

Chapters Three and Four: The Repeal of the Byrd and Clark Amendments

The carnage perpetrated by U.S. backed rebels in Angola and Mozambique has been a source of great concern to all those interested in bringing political stability to southern Africa. This chapter will, therefore, examine the roles, if any, played by religious groups in the struggle for the repeal of the Clark Amendment, which would allow the U.S. to send more military aid to the Angolan rebels. The efforts of relevant secular interest groups and the tactics they used will be analyzed.

Chapter Five: The Comprehensive Anti-Apartheid Act

Since this case involved the mass-mobilization of people and groups not seen since the civil rights and the anti-Vietnam War eras of the 1960s and 1970s, the activities, religious groups as well as important secular groups will be examined. The use of coalitional lobbying by religious and non-religious groups will also be noted.

Chapter Six: The Summary

This chapter will summarize the relevant findings of the research. It will examine whether the hypotheses posed in Chapter One have been proved or disproved by the study of the three cases of U.S. southern Africa policy. Suggestions as to how to more systematically study the activities and influence of religious groups in the shaping of U.S. southern Africa policy will be made. Areas for further research will be identified.

SIGNIFICANCE OF STUDY

One of the purposes of this investigation is to fill a research lacuna in the available literature on American interest groups and U.S. foreign policy. While scholars have traditionally analyzed the role and influence of both governmental and non-governmental interest groups on U.S. foreign policy, very little attempt has been made to systematically and comparatively study the influence of American religious groups in the shaping and implementation of U.S. foreign policy. Available studies of the impact of American religious groups on U.S. policy have often been hobbled by bias, contradictions, excessive caution, unsubstantiated generalizations, and abysmal ignorance of the role religions can and should play in forging a more just and humane American foreign policy.

Both Dahl and Almond exemplify the confusion among scholars as to the "proper" place and role of religious groups in the shaping of U.S. foreign policy. While one identifies a religious group as exercising foreign policy influence "out of all proportion to its size," the other sees religious leaders as incompetent actors in the American foreign policy process. This study will attempt to discover the empirical truth.

Among scholars, the role of religious groups as agents of political stability and change is equally controversial. Critics of religious as groups see the challenge of political change of their "Achilles heel," especially since they have historically been known to support the status quo. Such criticism, however, becomes specious, especially when it is realized that both Islam[145] and Christianity[146] can become agents of political change. This study, it is hoped, will contribute to a theory of religious groups and political change, especially as it relates to the African decolonization process.

Couloumbis and Wolfe have reiterated the importance of the study of religious groups:

> Assessing the role and political impact of religious groups in the late twentieth century, we find a wave of revitalization, revival, assertiveness, and activism. A recent example is the Iranian revolution, in which the clergy exercised power directly as well as indirectly. Few, also, can dispute the great impact and political consequences that a Pope's charismatic and authoritative pronouncements can have on important and controversial (hence political) issues such as population control, human rights, poverty, peace, and political liberalization. Further, the financial and political activities of American religious fundamentalists (operating under the rubric "moral majority") appear to have had a measurable impact in the 1980 American elections in support of conservative candidates.[147]

Finally, this investigation is no mere academic exercise. It is also a call for an "ecclesia-based" mobilization in America to correct certain historical wrongs. The Christian church[148] was a willing collaborator in the slave trade, in the colonization of Africa as well as an unwitting accomplice in the Jewish holocaust. The struggle against apartheid is an opportunity for the church to redress its historical sins of omission and commission in the fight for human rights. As citizens of the world's only economic and military superpower, American churches have by far a greater responsibility on global issues of justice and peace than any other group since such issues fall within the ethical/moral thoroughfare of their mission.

Hopefully, this study will help to arouse scholarly interest in American church groups as transnational actors with enormous potentialities for radically changing both the content and context of U.S. foreign policy not only in southern Africa but throughout the global community. Then, the ideals of the ancients enshrined in the sculpture at the U.N. would begin to be realized.

> In the days to come, the mountain of the Lord's house shall be established as the highest mountain...All nations shall stream toward it...He shall judge between the nations, and impose terms on many peoples. They shall beat their swords into plowshares and their spears into pruning hooks; One nation shall not raise the sword against another, nor shall they train for war again...[149]

SOURCES OF DATA

The data for this study will be selected from primary and secondary sources. Materials will be gathered primarily from the Archives of the United States Catholic Conference (USCC) and the National Council of Churches (NCC). These will be supplemented by information from several religious and lay group leaders, unstructured interviews and letter writing to some foreign policy makers.

Relevant books, magazines, secular, and religious journals and periodicals will also be used. The immense resources of the Library of Congress will be supplemented by those of Catholic, Howard, George Washington, American, and Georgetown universities. The resources of Brookings Institute, Institute of Policy Studies, American Enterprise Institute, and the Center for Strategic and International Studies, will be consulted.

BRIEF OVERVIEW OF CHURCH GROUPS

CATHOLICS - The United States Catholic Conference (U.S.C.C.)

The Roman Catholic Church in the U.S. is a branch of universal Catholicism. With a membership of 57,019,948,[150] American Catholics constitute the "largest church in the U.S."[151] The Church has 23,500 churches,[152] hundreds of colleges, universities, hospitals, and thousands of parochial schools. While its overall wealth still remains a mystery, in total assets, the U.S. Catholic Church is the richest church in America.[153]

The U.S.C.C. is the central bureaucracy of the Catholic Church in the U.S. It is a civil 'corporation related to the National Conference of Catholic Bishops (NCCB) in membership and directive control, but distinct from it in purpose and function.' The Official Catholic Directory states that the U.S.S.C. assists "the bishops in their service to the church in this country by uniting the people of God where voluntary collective action on a broad interdiocesan level is needed. The U.S.C.C. provides an organizational structure and the resources needed to insure coordination, cooperation, and assistance in the public, educational and social concerns of the church at the national and international level."[154] And, although it is a voluntary association to which each bishop adheres through choice and has no ecclesiastical jurisdiction or compulsory authority, it nonetheless, continues to 'exercise enormous influence.' On January 1, 1967, the U.S.C.C. had taken over the organization and operations of the former National Catholic Welfare Conference (NCWC), which was founded in 1917 as the National Catholic War Council.

Among the various divisions of the U.S.C.C. are the International Affairs and Justice and Peace Committees. The four-member Justice and Peace Committee opened an Africa division in 1975. It was run from 1975-1987 by a black priest, Fr. Rollins Lambert, who was succeeded by Mr. Dumas, an ex-U.S. diplomat with decades of experience in Africa. The annual budget of the Justice and Peace Committee in 1991 was $502,564, only 1.5% of the U.S.C.C. budget.[155] For 1992, it was $527,856, and 1.32% of the U.S.C.C.'s budget.[156]

NETWORK

In December 1971, forty-seven Catholic Sisters, horrified by the 'abominations of poverty they witnessed in the lives of people with whom they lived and worked,' met in Washington, DC and founded Network, a National Catholic Social Justice Lobby. It's purpose is "to influence Congress to enact laws providing economic justice for the poor, protecting human rights at home and abroad, promoting disarmament, are ensuring world peace."[157]

With a membership of over 8,000 and a budget of over $643,000, Network is the only registered Catholic lobby in Washington, DC.[158] Its members are found in every congressional district in the U.S. and are mostly made up of women religious. Unlike other non-registered religious lobbies, Network's lobbying efforts are virtually unlimited. The Washington Post states that 'Network has the reputation for being one of the most effective members of the religious lobby.' Barbara Mikulski (D-MD) concurred: "I have watched Network lobbying on many issues. They consistently are strong in support of all issues that are important to the dignity of women and men."[159]

Network also publishes Network Connection, a bi-monthly publication that "updates legislative issues, alerts you to take action at appropriate times, provides in-depth education and issue analysis, offers reflection on social justice theology and political ministry, and offers strategies for organizing and lobbying." According to the National Catholic Reporter,

> Network is looking at the moral implications and the social implications, of national legislation. Where Network is in opposition to that legislation, or some clause in it, the group acts as any political lobby would - it tries to muster enough clout to change legislation. Network is good news.[160]

PROTESTANTS - THE WASHINGTON OFFICE OF THE EPISCOPAL CHURCH

The Episcopal Church is the American branch of the world-wide Anglican communion. With less than 3 million members in 7,387 churches, the Episcopal Church is proof that strength is not always in numbers: "As a group, Episcopalians are by far the wealthiest, most Eastern, best educated, and most highly placed professionally of any christian denomination in the United States."[161] The Episcopal Church has also nine (9) colleges, one university, 6,745 nursery to high schools, and 43 hospitals.[162] It is "the semi-official church of America."[163]

Surprisingly the Episcopal Church did not have a Washington Office until 1979. And when it did, the office engaged in no lobbying. It was not until 1988 that the office was reorganized to "speak truth to the powers in Congress."

Established by the General Convention of the Episcopal Church, the main purpose of the Washington Office is to "bring the Resolutions of the Episcopal Church to the attention of our national policy makers [and] to open the line of communication between our elected officials and the Episcopal community."[164] This is done by arranging regular meetings 'between the staff of the Washington Office, Congressional Representatives, Senators, staff, and members of the Executive Branch and to assist members of the Episcopal Church and the world-wide Anglican Communion to speak directly to Members of Congress.' Finally, the Washington Office serves as a "resource for information," to provide 'timely information to encourage members to initiate their own advocacy efforts in response to the General Convention and Executive Council Resolutions.'

The Washington Office has a staff of four persons and a budget of $250,000. It's director is Rev. Robert J. Brooks.

THE WASHINGTON OFFICE ON AFRICA (WOA)

The Washington Office on Africa was set up in 1972 by the Presbyterian Church (U.S.A.), the Episcopal Church, the United Church of Christ, the United Methodist Church, and the African Committee on Africa (ACOA) as an anti-apartheid group. Its mission is to "coordinate, link and promote American and African grass roots agenda that affect public policies in the U.S. which support peace and political and economic justice in Africa."[165]

With a staff of four persons and a budget of $155,000, the WOA also acts as a resource center for and the legislative arm of various American church groups on African-related issues. Its first director was Rev. Edgar Lockwood. The WOA is presently run by the Assistant Director, Imani Countess.

THE UNITED CHURCH OF CHRIST (UCC)

The United Church of Christ (U.C.C.) consists of four churches which merged in 1961. They are the Congregational, Christian, Evangelical Synod and Reformed churches. With 1,625,969 members in 6,388 churches[166] who contribute $77,456,861 [167] annually, the U.C.C. is one of the most progressive churches in the U.S.

The Office of Church in Society (OCIS), established by the Tenth General Synod as the successor to the Council for Christian Social Action and the Center for Social Action, was mandated "to assume leadership function for social action concerns in the United Church of Christ, to provide resources to national Conferences and local churches and to strengthen coordination of social activities within the denomination."[168] The OCIS, which maintains a Washington, DC office, began to function on July 1, 1976. The Washington, DC office operates on behalf of the whole church

> to monitor legislation, to keep the whole church informed of public policy as it is being formed, and to pay particular attention to the development of legislation on which General Synod has taken a stand, so that the voice of the church may be heard effectively in turning what it believes into public policy.[169]

It has a staff of five persons and shares with the OCIS headquarters in Cleveland, Ohio, its $1 million budget. The Commission for Racial Justice has also been a major critic of U.S. Southern Africa policy. Its former Executive Director, Rev. Dr. Benjamin Chavis, was the head of the NAACP.

THE UNITED METHODIST CHURCH (UMC)

The present United Methodist Church is a product of two mergers. The first merger took place in 1939, when the Methodist and Episcopal Methodist churches were united. The second was in 1968 when the Methodist and Evangelical Brethren churches were merged to form the United Methodist Church (U.M.C.)[170] With a membership of 8,979,139 in 37,514[171] churches, it is the largest Methodist body in the U.S. In 1988, total contributions to the church was $569,125, 858.[172] Excluding its 101 colleges and universities, hospitals, plants, and homes, U.M.C. church property is worth about $17.5 billion.[173]

Two units of the U.M.C. are relevant to this study. They are the General Board of Church and Society (GBCS) and the Women's Division of the United Methodist General Board of Global Ministries, Washington office. The GBCS is the successor to the Methodist Board of Temperance and Public Morals and the premier social action agency of the church. It has a 92-member board of directors and a staff of 40 persons. The GBCS has a budget of about $1 million and "executes policies determined at United Methodist quadrennial conventions..."[174] Most of its budget, however, is spent on administration and constituency services.

The Women's Division of the U.M.C., Washington office, is a branch of the General Board of Global Ministries. Having operated for several decades under various names, it was restructured in its present form in 1972 into two divisions: 'the Office of Public Policy, which deals with legislative advocacy and constituency education, and the Office of Women's Concerns, which engages in research, consciousness raising, program development, and coordination on issues of women's concerns.' It has a staff of four persons and a budget of $350,000.

CHAPTER III - THE REPEAL OF THE BYRD AMENDMENT

While the main focus of this chapter is the repeal of the Byrd Amendment, there will also be an examination of the interplay of events and actors that gave birth to the Byrd Amendment per se. Thus, this chapter will be divided into four parts. The first part gives the historical background of Rhodesia prior to the Unilateral Declaration of Independence (UDI) by Ian Smith. It is primarily an examination of proto and subsequent African resistance to European colonialism. The second part examines the roles played by individuals and groups in the enactment of the Byrd Amendment. The third part identifies and examines relevant church groups, their policy preferences, tactics, and resources used in the struggle to repeal the Byrd Amendment. The fourth section is the concluding comment.

Background

The country that is today known as Zimbabwe was originally inhabited by various African ethnic groups before the advent of European colonialism. Among these were the Shona, the Urozwi, and others.[175] The Matabele, a Zulu-speaking people, having fled the wrath of Chaka, the great South African king, arrived in the country around 1835.[176]

On the one hand, Zimbabwe's colonial history was not unlike that of most African countries. It was a litany of deceit and conceit, invasion and confrontation, and subjugation and oppression of the indigenous African population.

On the other hand, Zimbabwe's colonial experience was unlike that of most African countries. In the majority of African countries under colonial rule, the colonial system was totally controlled by a relatively small cadre of white bureaucrats who were guided from their respective metropolitan capitals. In Rhodesia, a sizable settler community was unjustifiably allowed to exercise total domination over the African majority ab initio. Consequently, like in Algeria, Namibia, and the Portuguese colonies, the white settler presence in Rhodesia led to a degree of resistance and violence unknown in most African countries without a European settler presence.

African resistance to European colonialism in Rhodesia may be divided into four periods: proto-nationalism, collaborative politics, modern nationalism, and armed struggle.

The first stage of African resistance to European colonialism is the period of proto-nationalism which began with the Portuguese invasion in 1514.[177] Applying the strategy of divide et impera (divide and rule), the latter had succeeded in conquering portions of the country. They came for God, gold, and glory. Missionary groups, especially the Jesuits, were important actors on Portuguese colonial strategy, often acting as "advance troops" of the imperial enterprise. The initial success of the invaders in colonization was not merely due to their overwhelming military and technological supremacy. The disunity among the major indigenous African groups was also a major contributing factor.

Nonetheless, like other European colonial powers in Africa, Portuguese invasion of Rhodesia was violently resisted by the Africans ab initio. This resistance was successful in 1613, when the Mashonas, who had hitherto fought the Portuguese alone, formed an alliance with other African groups to expel the Europeans from their country.[178]

The Portuguese had to face the combined forces of Mwanamutapa, and Urozwi, for a new Mwanamutapa, Kamharapasu Mukumbwe had invited the Urozwi ruler, Chamgamire Dombo, to attack the Portuguese garrisons at Dambassa and elsewhere. Dombo lost no time. His regiment swept down on the Portuguese outposts. The inhabitants of these fled to Tete and Sena.[179]

The defeat of the Portuguese by an indigenous African army put paid to a lie traditionally propagated by apologists of European colonialism: That Africans could not and did not mount any credible resistance to early European invasions of their countries. Moreover, when such resistance was grudgingly acknowledged, these apologists often credited African military acumen to foreign influences--either to Arab-Moslem influences as was the case with the victory of the Sudanese Madhi over British General Gordon at the Siege of Omdurman in 1884[180] or the triumph of the Ethiopians over the Italians at the Battle of Adowa in 1896. In West Africa, African resistance was no less dogged and credible. In Ghana, the Ashantis fought the British for almost a hundred years in eleven major wars, all of which it won with the exception of one.[181] In Nigeria, King Jaja, the "Merchant Prince of West Africa," challenged British colonialism only to be forced into exile in the Caribbean in 1885.[182] He died in exile.

> The prime significance of African history becomes still more manifest when it is realized that this deliberate denial of African history arose out of the European expansion and invasion of Africa which began in the middle of the fifteenth century. The compulsion was thereby felt to attempt to justify such colonialist conquest, domination, enslavement, and plunder...[183]

The second group of Europeans to invade Zimbabwe were the British. They came in 1890 when London sent white settlers under the British South African Company (BSAC) to colonize Rhodesia. Following the so-called 'Rudd Concessions' deceptively obtained from Lobengula, King of the Matabele, Cecil Rhodes led his 'Pioneer Column' into the country as part of a strategy not only to dominate Africa but "for the bringing of the whole 'civilized' world under British rule, the recovery of the United States, and the making of an Anglo-Saxon race but one empire."[184] Rhodes also believed in the innate superiority of the Nordic stock and of the English among the Nordics. "We are the first race in the world," he boasted, "and the more the world we inhabit, the better it is for the human race."[185] Moreover, he saw Rhodesia as a British settler colony, a stop on his dream of the Cape to Cairo route.

Thus, from the outset, British policy exacerbated racial tension in Rhodesia, as it had earlier done in South Africa, from where the settlers came. The African majority was forced into a subordinate position vis-a-vis the white minority. They were discriminated against socially, politically, and economically.[186]

> On the assumption that Southern Rhodesia would ultimately become part of a South African federation and would therefore follow the pattern of the white 'dominions' the area was thrown open to white settlement, and the settlers soon had considerable powers devolved on them by the imperial authorities.[187]

Consequently, just as their ancestors had resisted Portuguese colonialism about three centuries earlier, the Africans, in a series of battles and uprisings, demonstrated their opposition to British takeover of their country.

The Matabeles were the first Africans to confront British imperial designs on Rhodesia. Granted that in the early 1890's, Lobengula, King of the Matabeles, did enter into some unequal and controversial treaties with the white settlers in an effort to satisfy their gargantuan territorial appetites, his opposition to British colonialism in Rhodesia was unmistakable. Vividly describing the rapacious nature of European colonialism, the wise and beleaguered king once observed:

> Did you ever see a chameleon catch a fly?...The chameleon gets behind the fly and remains motionless for sometime; then he advances very slowly and gently, first putting forward one leg and then another. At last, when well within reach, he darts his tongue and the fly disappears. England is the chameleon and I am the fly.[188]

Reiterating his opposition to the increasing white settler presence in his country, Lobengula once told a missionary: "But the Queen must not let too many of her people come. That I will not allow. I have been told the English are never content with their own country, but must needs go into other peoples. Tell the Queen my words."[189]

But the British had their designs on Rhodesia. After several provocations and standoffs, war finally broke out between the Matabele and the British on October 22, 1893.[190] Both sides were unequally matched. By 1894, the 'logic of the gun' had given victory to the small white settler group over the numerically superior but technologically inferior impis (soldiers) of Lobengula's army. Flush in victory, Rhodes addressed the settlers: "You will be the first entitled to select land...It is your right, for you have conquered the country."[191]

But the period of African proto-nationalism in Rhodesia was not yet over. In 1896, as the Rhodesian white settler army was attacking the Boer republics of Transvaal and Orange Free States during the Jameson Raid, a joint Shona-Matabele force seized the opportunity to attack the European settlers in their midst. Many whites were killed and their property destroyed. And, even though the 1893 and 1896 African uprisings, which are called the first 'chimurenga' or war of liberation, were brutally put down by the British, the Africans had shown their mettle on the battlefield. According to John G. Jackson,

> Until near the end of the nineteenth century the African freedom struggle was a military struggle. This aspect of African history has been shamefully neglected. I do not believe the neglect is an accident. African oppressors and Western historians are not ready to concede the fact that Africa has a fighting heritage. The Africans did fight back and they fought exceptionally well... This fight was led, in most cases, by African kings... These revolutionary nationalist African kings are mostly unknown because the white interpreters of Africa still want the world to think that the African waited in darkness for other people to bring the light.[192]

The combined effort of the Shonas and the Matabele to expel the Europeans from their country was inspired by the 'Cult' of Mwari or traditional African religion and its mediums. The "Nehanda and Kagubi" spirit mediums were used to invoke the Shona tradition of resistance aga Until near the end of the nineteenth century the African freedom struggle was a military struggle. This aspect of African history has been shamefully neglected. I do not believe the neglect is an accident. Africa's oppressors and Western historians are not ready to concede the fact that Africa has a fighting heritage. The Africans did fight back and they fought exceptionally well...This fight was led, in most cases, by African kings...These revolutionary nationalist African kings are mostly unknown because the white interpreters of Africa still want the world to think that inst invaders.[193] The messages and directives of the mediums were seen as orders from Mwari (God).[194] In Julius Caesar, Shakespeare observes that 'fire is used to drive out fire.' In Zimbabwe, just as European colonialism was often driven by the fire of the christian faith, African proto-nationalism was equally driven by the fire of traditional African religion.

The victory of European colonialism in Zimbabwe traumatized the Africans. Like the Europeans during the 'Dark Ages,' the Africans sought to ride out of the crisis of their defeat by looking back to their past. In a certain sense, nations are not unlike individuals, in crisis, they retreat to their roots to rediscover and fortify themselves to regain a measure of equilibrium. In Rhodesia, the two major African groups sought a Zimbabwean renaissance in two different ways. The Matabeles sought the restoration of the monarchy through Lobengula's children. For that purpose, they inaugurated the Loyal Mandebele Patriotic Society in 1915, which called for "higher education, the growth of the African church, the autonomy of a black race and the need for unity."[195] The African Methodist Episcopal Church of South Africa (AMEC), which had a school in the country, was very influential in the organization.[196] However, the Mandebele Patriotic Society was too pro-British, and was therefore, of no significance in the anti-colonial struggle.

The Mashonas followed a more traditional approach. They invoked the memory of their national hero, Nehanda, now reincarnated in the prophetess Chainuka, and hoped she would lead them to freedom.

> In 1906, a female spirit medium appeared in Mazoe for the spirit of Nehanda. She was the first medium to appear since the execution of the Nehanda medium who lead the 1896 uprising in Mazoe and the administration was understandingly anxious about her.[197]

But the Mashona anti-colonial strategy was equally suppressed.

In fact, the first Africans to voice any organized opposition against the colonial system in Rhodesia were not the indigenous Africans. Rather, they were the "Black Pioneers," the "colonial boys," or "alien natives," South Africans, who had fought on the side of the British against the Mashona and Matabele in the wars of 1893 and 1896.[198] They were used by Rhodes to form a 'cordon sanitaire' of loyal Africans to counteract the indigenous population, and were mostly christian. They were the African equivalent of "house blacks" in the U.S. during the era of slavery in that they were the favored group among the Africans. But by 1905, the colonial regime had disarmed them and excluded them from the military; the white settlers no longer made any distinctions between them and other black Zimbabweans. Dumped by their former masters and hated by indigenous Zimbabweans, the 'colonial boys' were caught in the middle. In response, they formed their own organizations, the Union of South African Native Associations and the Union Natives Vigilance Association,[199] to fight for their rights. They were influenced in their struggle by their kith and kin in South Africa, especially by the independent churches there which came to Zimbabwe and became militantly anti-European.[200] By the end of the first World War, the South Africans were identifying themselves as Zimbabweans. The absorption of the former 'colonial boys' into the black Zimbabwean population was so total that after the formation of the ANC in South Africa in 1912, it became the mouthpiece of both the South African and Zimbabwean struggles against white minority rule in both countries.[201]

The second stage in the anti-colonial struggle in Rhodesia may be described as the era of "collaborative politics." It was also the epoch of the "mission boys." With the failure of the Zimbabwean renaissance, many Africans now sought salvation in the christian churches which, they believed, would liberate if not their bodies, at least, their souls. Prominent among these churches were Matthew Chigaga Zvimba's "Church of the White Bird," which regarded those killed in 1896-97 war as "saints and martyrs of the new church"[202] and the more powerful John Charafambira's Vapasiton church, which was anti-white.[203]

Many Africans also joined European and American missionary churches. In fact, most of the "mission boys" were products of these churches. Drawn from different ethnic groups but sharing a common mission experience, they were the first to form supra-ethnic associations like the Rhodesian Bantu Voters Association and the Rhodesia Native Association in the early 1920s.[204] Most members of these organization were Matabele. Around the same time, the Rhodesia Native Association, a predominantly Shona group, was founded. All these associations were conservative; and even though they often expressed their opposition to the harsher aspects of white settler rule, they were, nevertheless, pro-British to the core. Generally, their leaders, the "mission boys," were mostly Westernized African elites, who preferred to work within the colonial system, hoping that their strategy would, in the long run, lead Africans to a position where they would be able to share power with whites in a parliamentary system. By 1934, these elites had formed the Southern Rhodesia African National Congress, an elitist and reformist political party modelled after the ANC. The merger of the City Youth League (CYL), founded in 1955, with the ANC in 1957, did not detract the new organization from its "unfailing loyalty to the British Crown."[205] As Ndabaningi Sithole has observed,

the African politician may turn his nose up in derision, and twist his lips
by way of deprecation when he hears it said that the christian church
laid secure foundations for African nationalism... The christian church
may be regarded in one sense as the spiritual father, whether or not
the church recognizes the role...Practically all important African
political leaders went through the christian church school.[206]

All the same, the type of nationalism advocated by the "mission
boys" during the period of "collaborative politics" was defective. Its
limitations were especially evident in the fate of the Federation of the
Rhodesias and Nyasaland.[207]   As other African countries became
independent, it was obvious that the days of white minority rule in
southern Africa were doomed. However, the role of some of the
churches continued to be ambivalent. By the 1960s, many of the
churches and African nationalism became mutually incompatible.[208]

The third stage in the anti-colonial struggle was the era of modern
African nationalism. Its origin may be traced to the formation of the
National Democratic Party (NDP) on January 1, 1960 and was a point
of departure in Rhodesian politics. For the first time, blacks abandoned
their routine pledge of loyalty to the British Crown and demanded
instead the establishment of a democratic government based on one-
man, one-vote.[209] By December, 17, 1961, Joshua Nkomo had formed
the Zimbabwe People's Union (ZAPU) to replace the NDP.[210] Like the
NDP, ZAPU was ideological, anti-colonial, and anti-imperialist. But
it was, however, opposed to the use of armed struggle in the liberation
of Rhodesia. Rather, ZAPU promoted the concept of PanAfricanism in
its efforts to win financial and moral support from sympathetic African
countries.[211] Nonetheless, ZAPU was banned in September 1962 by
the settler regime in Rhodesia.

Due to serious internal problems, ZAPU experienced a division
within its ranks. On August 8, 1963, a group of dissidents led by Rev.
Ndabaningi Sithole formed the Zimbabwe African National Union
(ZANU).[212] Although ZANU was allegedly more militant than ZAPU,
its adoption of the armed struggle was more of a device to elicit British
intervention in Rhodesia rather than an outright support of liberation
through armed violence. Consequently, it was not until after the feeble
British and African response to UDI that ZANU was finally convinced
that it was only through armed struggle that an independent Zimbabwe
would come into being.[213]

The fourth stage of the anti-colonial struggle in Rhodesia is the
recourse to armed violence by African nationalist guerrillas, also

known as the "second chimurenga" or second war of liberation. It was provoked by an incident without precedent in the history of British colonialism in Africa: the unilateral declaration of Rhodesia's independence (UDI) by Ian Smith on November 11, 1965.[214]

Since the first chimurenga of the late 19th century had been mercilessly crushed by the white settlers, what chances had the second chimurenga to succeed? Several factors contributed to the second war of liberation. Among these were the changing international environment, a growing militance among the internal opponents of UDI, and, most importantly, the recourse by African nationalists to armed violence.

The changing international attitude toward Rhodesia is evident from the reactions of Britain and other important international organizations to UDI. After five years of stalling and inaction, Prime Minister Harold Wilson warned Ian Smith that his government would do all that was needed to "restore Rhodesia to the rule of law, to allegiance to the crown."[215]

At the OAU foreign ministers' meeting in Addis Ababa, a resolution warned that unless Britain crushed the rebellion and "restores law and order, and thereby prepare the way for majority rule in Southern Rhodesia, member-states of the OAU shall sever diplomatic relations with the United Kingdom."[216] A committee of five was appointed to reconvene with military advisers from the OAU to 'study and plan the use of force to assist the people of Zimbabwe.' In the long run, however, only Tanzania and Ghana broke diplomatic relations with Britain because of UDI.[217] Other than the provision of military material and advice, neither the OAU as a body nor any individual African country was willing to use its own military to crush the rebel regime in Rhodesia.

On December 16, 1966, more than one year after UDI, the U.N. adopted a British-sponsored resolution that condemned the Smith regime for constituting a "threat to international peace," and imposed on it selective sanctions.[218] On March 29, 1968, the U.N. imposed mandatory sanctions and embargo on trade with the white minority regime.[219]

The response of both the U.N. and Britain fell far short of African expectations. For whereas the former went to war in the 1950's to stop "communist aggression" in Korea, and the latter had no qualms in crushing the so-called Mau-Mau Freedom-Fighters in colonial Kenya, neither was prepared to use military force in Rhodesia. The feeble response of Great Britain in particular reveals the rank racism and hypocrisy characteristic of European colonialism in Africa. It also lends credence to the adage: blood is thicker than water. For if the roles were reversed, would Britain have watched helplessly as a black African minority oppressed a white majority? In holy anger, would not they and other European countries have intervened as the French and the Belgians have often done in Zaire?

The success of the second chimurenga was, therefore, not a product of external non-African intervention. It was primarily the work of African nationalist guerrillas who were forced by UDI to understand the full import of Frederick Douglas' words: "Power concedes nothing without demand. It never has; it never will." "Within one year, the first armed attack on the Rhodesian state since the 1896 rebellion (the first chimurenga) took place. It was carried out near the town of Sinoia by a small group of guerrillas belonging to the Zimbabwe African National Union (ZANU). It would take 14 years before majority rule would be achieved."[220] While the attack at Sinoia was mostly a failure, it was nonetheless, a warning to Salisbury that African nationalists were ready and willing to use armed violence if necessary to win their freedom. In their struggle, the African guerrillas, most of whom were baptized christians, surprisingly, had powerful allies not in the cross or the Madonna, but in the spirit mediums, prophets, and custodians of traditional African rituals and culture and the guarantors of the peoples' freedom. Perhaps the most famous of the mediums was Mazoe Nehanda, a major woman leader of the 1896 rebellion against colonialism. It was to another woman, a "reincarnation" of Nehanda, that the guerrillas now prayed for the liberation of their country:

Where is our Freedom, Nehanda? Won't you come down to help us? Our old men are treated like children. In the land you gave them, merciful Creator.[221]

Within Rhodesia, African response to UDI was equally unsuccessful. Strikes, protest marches, and unorganized violence were brutally put down by the white minority regime.[222] But outside the country, the failure at Sinoia forced both ZAPU and ZANU to send their cadres to be trained in Ghana, China, the Soviet Union, Cuba, Algeria, and other countries. At Dori Camp, Zimbabwean refugees vowed: "I have given my life to liberate Zimbabwe. I am going to finish the work left incomplete by our great-grand-parents. I shall sleep in the mountains and in the streams till Zimbabwe is free.[223]"

THE ROLE OF NON-CHURCH GROUPS

The second part of the study examines the various factors that made the enactment of the Byrd Amendment of 1971 possible. These include various individuals and groups who, by their action and inaction, expedited the breaking by the U.S. of the only mandatory and comprehensive sanctions program ever voted into the U.N. charter. These factors may be divided into reactions by Congressmen, interest groups, the White House, and other executive agencies.

Opposition to sanctions against the Ian Smith regime did not begin with the introduction of the Byrd Amendment. It can be traced to the Senate when James Eastland (D-Mississippi) introduced a resolution in 1966 calling for an end to American economic measures against Southern Rhodesia.[224] By 1969, several anti-sanctions resolutions had been introduced in the House. In 1970, Eastland sponsored S. Res 376 which sought the restoration of trading relations with and the recognition of the illegal Smith regime.[225] The rationale for this resolution was that sanctions had forced the U.S. to become dependent on the Soviet Union for a strategic mineral, chrome ore. In the same year, six resolutions advocating the violation of sanctions were introduced in the House. But congressional reaction to these resolutions were at that time, weak.

By 1971, however, when ten conservative congressmen introduced anti-sanctions bill, congressional interest in the violation of sanctions by the U.S. had increased. On February 22, 1971 Congressman James Collins (R-Texas) introduced HR 4712, "a bill to amend the United Nations Participation Act of 1945 to prevent the imposition thereunder of any prohibition on the importation of like ore from any communist country is not prohibited by law."[226] By March 3, 1971, Collins had changed the phrase "any metal bearing ore" to "strategic and critical," and, thus, turned it into a national-security and economic issue. On March 29, 1971, Senator Harry F. Byrd (Ind-Va) introduced a similar bill in the Senate, S. 1404.[227]The "Byrd Amendment" was born. However, after hearings in both the House Subcommittee on International Organizations and Movements and the Senate Foreign Relations Committee in June and July respectively, both chambers rejected Byrd's bill.

But Senator Byrd was undaunted. Having failed in the two committees, he attached his bill, now renamed Section 503, as an amendment to the Military Procurement Act, which had already been passed in the House and was then being considered by the Senate Armed Services Committee. It had the support of a powerful group of 'Leviathans,' the southern senators who controlled some of the most important committees in Congress. Attempts by Senators McGee and Fulbright to kill the amendment were unsuccessful, each failing by ten and six votes respectively.

In the Conference Committee that followed, the amendment survived, especially because the majority of its members were conservative; moreover, since it already had the imprimatur of the Senate, it was difficult for House Committee members to reject it.

On November 10, 1971 when the conference report was sent to the House, Representative Donald Fraser, with the support of Representative Charles Diggs and others, offered an amendment to delete Section 503. It failed woefully by a vote of 251 to 100, and 80 members abstaining. The Senate passed the conference report the next day by a vote of 69 to 19, with 16 members not voting. And on November 17, 1971, Nixon signed the Military Procurement Authorization Bill, with Section 503 attached into law.[228]

The roles of the White House and other relevant executive departments in the enactment of the Byrd Amendment indicate the overall confusion pervading Nixon's policy toward Rhodesia. For, in spite of all the empty rhetoric and promises, the White House was no strong opponent of the amendment. First, before the passage of Byrd it refused to show an interest in the issue, either in official statements or through the activities of the White House staff or their political allies. Second, after the passing of the Byrd Amendment, the White House had promised McGee that it would call wavering Republican Senators to support a repeal. It never kept its promise. "Let us keep one fact straight," Senator McGee angrily reiterated, "it is not the Congress who can now be blamed for its defeat. It is not the Foreign Relations Committee. It is not the steel companies or the steel workers' unions. The White House, for whatever reasons, chose not to try to win this one."[229]

On their own, both the State Department and its Office of Congressional Relations opposed the anti-sanctions activities of Byrd and his compatriots. In their actions and public statements during the debate on the controversial amendment, the position of State was unmistakable. Assistant Secretary of State Newsome and other Department witnesses, who testified in various hearings held by the

Senate Foreign Relations and the House Foreign Affairs Subcommittees, condemned the anti-sanctions amendment. In fact, between the passage of Byrd in October, 1971 and the failed attempt at repeal in May 31, 1972, the State Department did issue some of the strongest statements against the amendment. On May 20, 1972, John Urwin, II, then Acting Secretary of State, sent a strongly worded letter to Senator McGee in which he reaffirmed the administration's support for repeal: "Repeal would serve to make us less vulnerable to unfavorable international reaction. As a result of the legislation now in force, our international interests have suffered in other respects. In Africa, where our position on Rhodesia has heretofore been seen as a test of our commitment to self-determination and racial equality, our credibility has suffered..."[230]

But the State Department did not only release statements, it also actively lobbied for a continuation of sanctions. On May 14, and June 17, 1971, David Abshire, the Assistant Secretary of State for Congressional Relations, sent letters to the Chairman of the House Foreign Affairs Committee stating his opposition to Byrd. Michael Samuels, a hard working member of the Office of Congressional Relations, was asked to work full-time against Byrd, providing swing vote senators with speaking materials and calling congressional offices. All the same, State used only low-ranking officials to lobby against the Byrd Amendment. Neither Secretary of State William Rogers nor any of his high-ranking subordinates lobbied for a continuation of sanctions. At the National Security Council, neither Henry A. Kissinger nor the NSC staff cared about the amendment or made any attempts to have a positive influence on the sanctions issue.

From the beginning, several interest groups sought to influence the outcome of the Rhodesian sanctions controversy. These groups may be divided into the anti- and pro-sanctions supporters. The anti-sanctions groups were predominantly corporate interests. They included Union Carbide, Foote Mineral, Corning Glass, the American Iron and Steel Institute (AISI), and the Tool and Stainless Steel Industry Committee. Foremost among the non-business anti-sanctions groups were the Rhodesian Information Office in Washington, D.C., right-wing groups like the Friends of Rhodesian Independence (an offshoot of the Liberty Lobby), the American-Southern Africa Council, the American African Affairs Association, Inc., and "some fundamentalist ministers and conservative elements in the major national churches."[231]

The pro-sanctions groups include the American Committees on Africa(ACOA), labor unions, churches,[232] African-American organizations, and Americans for Democratic Action. Unlike their opponents, they were ideologically more liberal.

Of all these groups, however, corporate interests were the most potent. They had the money, the connections, the zeal and the skills unmatched by the competition. Their primary interest was unmistakable. It was purely economic and seemed to have little regard for the moral dimension of white minority colonialism in Rhodesia. The overall attitude of these business groups was expressed by L.G. Bliss, president of Foote Mineral, when he called on the U.S. to base its Rhodesian policy on pragmatism instead of idealism. He also warned that the U.S. should be circumspect in adhering to the principles of international morality when American economic and security interests were at stake.[233]

Unlike the White House, however, the activities of the companies went beyond mere rhetoric. For example, in 1971, Union Carbide, Foote Mineral, and Allegheny Ludlum Steel lobbied heavily for the passage of HR5445 by which the House voted against Rhodesian sanctions. E.F. Andrews, a vice-president at Allegheny Ludlum Steel and a member of the Tool and Stainless Steel Industry Committee personally lobbied several congressman to support the anti-sanctions bill. He also appeared before several congressional hearings to defend the lifting of sanctions against the rebel enclave. The Washington, D.C. law firm of Collier, Shannon, Rill and Edwards was contracted by the company to coordinate its overall lobbying efforts over the sanctions issue. Indeed, the Tool and Stainless Steel Industry Committee was said to have "carried the ball" on the Byrd Amendment.[234] The American Iron and Steel Institute (AISI), which represented the American carbon steel manufacturers, also lobbied heavily against sanctions. According to James Collins, its regional vice-president in Washington, D.C., AISI lobbying activities against sanctions included the writing of letters to 60 Congressmen.

Senator Humphrey labelled the excessive influence of business groups over Congress' attitude toward sanctions as "twisting public policy for private interest."[235] Senator McGee concurred: "It is, indeed, a sad day when the U.S. Senate falls victim to a ploy as reprehensible as this and allows foreign policy considerations to be determined by two corporations who have significant holdings in Rhodesia."[236]

Coordinating the activities of the anti-sanctions forces in the U.S. was the Rhodesian Information Office (RIO) in Washington, the official agent of the Ian Smith regime in the country. Given America's original support of U.N. sanctions against Salisbury, the presence in the U.S. of representatives of the white minority regime was controversial, especially when the latter engaged in consular and political affairs. Spending about $171,000 per year, the RIO propaganda machine, which included the publication and distribution of the Rhodesian Commentary, Rhodesian Viewpoint, and Press Comment on Rhodesia, had as its main objective the creation of a pro-Rhodesian constituency in the U.S. The RIO also sought to influence U.S. public opinion through speaking tours, films, pictures, television, and radio shows promoting U.S. - Rhodesian relations. In the same vein, it was not unusual for officials of the RIO to attend congressional committee hearings, meet with Congressmen, Senators, and the media "at their request" to promote Rhodesians interests. The Rhodesia Information Service lobbied heavily and with great success on the Byrd Amendment.[237] To celebrate the passing of the Byrd Amendment, the RIO gave a Christmas party in which the song the "503 Club Marching Song" was sung to the tune of "O Tannenbaum:" "Oh, 503, oh, 503. We gave our very best for thee... We celebrate our victory. To Harry Byrd, we drink a toast...Jim Collins, too, we'll honor thee.."[238]

Confronting the pro-Rhodesian lobby in the U.S. were various anti-racist, anti-apartheid, anti-colonial and largely liberal interest groups. Among them, the American Committee on Africa (ACOA) was, arguably, the most active on the Rhodesian issue. Originally organized in 1953 to fight against colonialism in Africa and to influence U.S. policy, as most African countries became independent by the early 1960's, ACOA redirected its anti-colonial efforts to southern Africa, a region still controlled by colonial and white minority regimes. To achieve these ends, it published the Southern Africa Bulletin and Africa Today and engaged in other lobbying activities. From the very beginning, ACOA opposed UDI and supported sanctions against Rhodesia. It opposed the Byrd Amendment, but like other anti-Rhodesian groups,

> its efforts were sadly flawed, however, by its tardiness in becoming engaged. In mid-September, after the Armed Services Committee had reported Senator Byrd's Amendment on the floor, the New York headquarters of ACOA had not even heard of its existence. The head of ACOA's Washington office had gone on vacation after his

unsuccessful fight that summer to defeat the American sugar quota for
South Africa.[239]

Consequently, since the churches which had relied on the ACOA
for legislative information, were taken by surprise, they were "not an
important factor when the Byrd Amendment was passed in 1971."[240]

Among the labor unions that opposed the enactment of the Byrd
Amendment, the United Steel Workers of America played a prominent
role.   About one month before the passage of the amendment, it
provided pro-sanctions Congressmen with research materials
supporting the need for sanctions. Together with other unions, it also
mailed similar letters to them.   These actions were, somehow,
undermined by William A. Hart, a local trade unionist from
Pennsylvania who warned that the rejection of Byrd would lead to the
"destruction of specialty steel industry in Pennsylvania or the United
States."   Stating that Hart's views were neither sanctioned by the
executive board nor reflective of union position, I.W. Bell, the
president of the United Steel Workers, responded that the problems of
the specialty steel industry could be solved "not by breaking the
Rhodesian embargo on chrome ore."

No doubt, among the black leaders who led the fight against the
passing of the Byrd Amendment, Congressman Charles Diggs (D-
Michigan) stands out.   Supported by a coalition of over fifty
Congressmen, he showed his opposition to the amendment from the
very beginning. He not only testified against it, he influenced the views
of his fellow congressmen, especially those of the members of the
Congressional Black Caucus. On September 29, 1971, the Caucus had
sent a letter to Secretary of State Rogers and a telegram to Nixon
asking for their support against the Byrd Amendment. On his own
part, Mr. Diggs even tendered his resignation as a member of the
American delegation to the U.N. in late 1971, partly to protest U.S.
policy toward Salisbury. He presented five reasons to justify his
opposition to the Byrd Amendment.   First, the passage of the
amendment would not only violate American's international obligations
under the U.N. charger, it could seriously undermine her credibility as
a promoter of human rights and self-determination in Africa. Second,
the Byrd Amendment should not be seen as an economic and security
problem, but rather as one dealing primarily with the question of
African majority rule in Rhodesia. Third, if the amendment were to be
passed, it would be tantamount to a clear, calculated denial of our legal

obligations and of our duty as a U.N. member state to carry out the decisions of the Security Council. Fourth, sanctions were economically harmful to U.S. interests. Fifth, it would rather place the U.S. squarely on the side of the African majority in Rhodesia.

THE REPEAL OF THE BYRD AMENDMENT

After the enactment of the Byrd Amendment in 1971, a "new effort during 1973-1974 came very close to gaining its repeal."[241] This effort started in the Senate when twenty-three Senators co-sponsored a bill introduced by Senator Hubert Humphrey to repeal the amendment. On May 25, 1973, forty union representatives, including the powerful Steel Workers and the United Auto Workers (UAW), and over twenty-five other groups gathered to devise a strategy in support of repeal bills already in the Senate and House three days earlier.[242] At the meeting, it was agreed that a full-time staff to coordinate the groups' lobbying activities would be hired from the Washington Office on Africa (WOA). The prospect for repeal looked better in the Senate than in the House.

Statements of support for repeal came from leaders of various organizations. On May 23, 1973, UAW President Leonard Woodcock issued a strong statement of support for Rhodesian sanctions. On May 29, 1973, the Steel Workers sent letters to Congress in which they argued that repeal would not hurt their jobs. Resolutions supporting repeal came from the American Bar Association and the Oil, Chemical and Atomic Workers, which represents Union Carbide workers. With interests in Rhodesia, Union Carbide had lobbied strenuously for the enactment of the Byrd Amendment.

The Nixon administration also seemed to be opposed to the Byrd Amendment. On June 7, 1973, the U.S. representative to the U.N., Ambassador John Scali, called on Congress to repeal the amendment. At hearings on his nomination as Secretary of State on September 7, 1973, Henry Kissinger stated that the administration favored repeal.[243]

On September 18, 1973, the Senate Foreign Relations Committee "favorably reported Humphrey's bill to the floor, by voice vote and without dissent." When the bill came to the full Senate, a filibuster by Senator Harry Byrd was initially successful. But after intensive lobbying by the White House, the State Department, telegrams from constituents, and the political astuteness of Senators Hubert Humphrey and McGee, cloture was voted on December 18, 1973 and Humphrey's bill passed by 63 to 26 votes.[244]

In the House, a different story emerged. In spite of support for repeal by the Ford administration, the New York Times, The Los Angeles Times, and The Baltimore Sun, the repeal effort was stalled in the House for about two years. And when the Byrd Amendment was voted upon on September 25, 1975, the House rejected repeal by a vote of 187 to 209.[245]

The victory of Carter over Ford in 1976 sent promise and impetus to the repeal effort in Congress. With the collapse of the Geneva talks on Rhodesia's independence, its British and American sponsors knew that until the Byrd Amendment was repealed, neither Smith nor the African nationalists would take the U.S. position on majority rule seriously. Repeal was intended to convince the Rhodesian authorities that "under no circumstances can they count on any form of American assistance in preventing majority rule or in engineering a settlement which excludes nationalist leaders."[246] For Andrew Young, "repeal of the Byrd Amendment is a kind of referendum on American racism. It is viewed that way by the heads of states of the black majority nations."[247] Consequently, with strong support from the White House and little opposition from the steel industry, the Byrd Amendment was easily repealed by votes of 250-146 in the House on March 14, 1977 and 86-26 in the Senate on March 16.[248]

CHURCH GROUPS

The third part of this chapter identifies and examines church groups, their policy preferences, resources, and tactics used in the struggle to repeal the Byrd Amendment. Like the secular interest groups, the enactment of anti-Rhodesian sanctions legislation took American church interest groups by surprise. However, as soon as they awoke from their slumber, they were quick in organizing opposition to the amendment. Of these groups, the United Methodist Church, the Washington Office on Africa and the United Church of Christ were prominent. The United States Catholic Conference was also involved in the pro-sanctions campaign. By both their statements and actions, U.S. Catholic and Protestant groups showed their opposition to the Byrd Amendment and their support for the restoration of sanctions against the white minority regime in Rhodesia.

PROTESTANTS

Among opponents of the Byrd Amendment, the WOA probably played the most important role in the ensuing battle over the repeal of the controversial amendment. In October, 1975, it condemned the September 25, defeat in the House of an attempt to restore U.S. compliance with sanctions against Rhodesia: "The vote of 187 to 209, which came on only one week's notice, was a disheartening culmination to almost three years of effort in support of sanctions by Africa liberation supports groups, church and civil rights groups, labor unions and Congressional sponsors. The defeat of HR1287 almost certainly destroys any possibility that Congress will renew full U.S. compliance with sanctions against Rhodesia during this session."[249] It condemned the attitude of supporters of the amendment as "a classic example of the use of anti-communism and racism to cloud the interests of U.S. industries seeking profits from the exploitation of developing countries."[250] On March 29, 1976, the WOA called the rapidly changing situation "the most critical issue the United States is now facing."[251] Stating that the white minority regime in Salisbury would be unable to defeat a united African nationalist military force, it found the reaction of the Ford administration to the possibility of black African victory alarming: "Secretary Kissinger is bent on proving that U.S. withdrawal from Angola will not be a precedent for the region. Direct support for the white minority regime on the battlefield is still politically unfeasible, but Kissinger seems to seriously believe that military action against Cuba for any assistance to the Zimbabwe nationalist forces is not."[252] And in the summer of 1978, the WOA bemoaned the conservative mood in Congress, which led to the Case/Javits Compromise. The Compromise made the repeal of the Byrd Amendment conditional. According to the WOA, the Carter administration lost the vote in Congress because it "had reinforced the anti-communism on which the right-wing based its support for the internal settlement and attack on the patriotic front..."[253]

But the actual struggle to repeal the Byrd Amendment started earlier in April 1972 when Diggs, the Black Caucus, and their allies had filed a complaint in the U.S. District Court for the District of Columbia against the Secretary of the Treasury, government officials, and others basically seeking the overturn of the Byrd Amendment.[254] The repeal movement gathered added momentum with the appointment in May of Rev. Ted Lockwood, a lawyer and Episcopal priest, as the director of the new WOA organization. Rev. Lockwood, a former civil rights activist, saw the Byrd Amendment as a blight on U.S. African policy and resolved to help in its reversal by utilizing the resources of the WOA. With a permanent staff of five persons and financial support from sympathetic churches and individuals who feared that Rhodesia would become another Vietnam, the WOA went on the offensive. A key member of the staff was Leslie Yates, who became an aide to Congressman Diggs.

From 1973 to 1974, Congressional opponents of the Byrd Amendment and their supporters made serious efforts to repeal the regressive legislation. The WOA was an important player in this struggle. Its efforts received a boost in December 1972, when members of the United Steel Workers of America came to Rev. Lockwood with a story that would radically affect the issue of Rhodesian sanctions: Rhodesian chrome was coming into the U.S. and U.S. chrome workers were being put out of business.[255] With this information, the Rhodesian sanctions imbroglio, which was, for many years, viewed by many Americans as a far-away problem involving a remote part of Africa, was suddenly injected into the domestic politics of the U.S. in the powerful and emotional language of "job creation and job loss." It was the type of information that could change the vote of a wavering politician, especially if he had steel mills in his district. Most striking about the way lobbyists spend their time "is the premium they place on collecting the latest information. Close attention is paid to relevant sources of news."[256]

Armed with this information, the WOA went to Congress and asked that the debate on the amendment be reopened. After meeting with sympathetic Congressman Don Fraser (D-Mn), who succeeded in recruiting co-sponsors in the House, there was hope that repeal was possible. From June to September, 1973, the WOA met several times with Fraser's staff in strategy sessions. During these sessions, the Congressional staffers, who are normally in touch daily with their Congressmen, told WOA what arguments to use in their meetings with their boss. In return, they received the latest information on the Rhodesian crisis from a group, which often had more up-to-date information, given its unique links to the troubled region. But, in spite of all its efforts, the repeal effort failed in the House on November 10, 1971, by twenty-two votes.

Initially, the Senate looked more auspicious, especially since the repeal effort was sponsored by the powerful liberal Senator Humphrey and the conservative Senator McGee. Earlier, the WOA had met both men and asked for their assistance in the repeal effort.

While other forms of lobbying are recommended, no tactic is considered more effective by lobbyists than personally presenting their case to a Congressman in a private meeting because a meeting with a legislator is an opportunity to press the case home and make him or her truly understand the virtue of the group's position.[257]

WOA also held strategy sessions with key members of the two senators' staffs. For example, such sessions were held with Dan Spiegle, an aide to Senator Hubert Humphrey, and Dick McCoy, Senators McGee's assistant, from June to September 1973. An important tactic that emerged out of these sessions was that the WOA should target and analyze congressional districts with sizeable black populations and to encourage them to pressure their congressmen to support Rhodesian sanctions. Steel workers were contacted and reminded of the danger the importation of Rhodesian chrome posed to their jobs. This was also the tactic used by Chrysler during the famous Chrysler bailout. After Lee Iacocca, chairman of Chrysler, had presented his company's problems to Tip O'Neal, he said:

Tell me, how many people in my district work for Chrysler or one of its suppliers?" "I have no idea," he replied. "Find out," I told him. "That's the key to this thing. And do the same for every district in the country. Make up a list, and have your employees and dealers in each district call and write letters to their own member of Congress. You've heard my famous phrase that all politics is local. A lot of jobs will be lost if Chrysler goes under, and believe me, no member wants to see something like that happen in his district.[258]

The WOA also employed congressional hearings, group visits, letter-writing campaigns, telephone and telegrams to pressure Congress to reverse the Byrd Amendment. In this exercise, the Northeast and the West Coast were more favorable to WOA's efforts. Southern states were less receptive to the organization. However, by the time the Byrd Amendment was repealed in 1977, the sanctions campaign had helped WOA to grow from a national membership of fifty people to three thousand. An important contribution to this growth may have been Mr. Edwin ("Ned") Crosby from Minnesota, who gave WOA $36,000 to facilitate the sanctions drive.[259] Mr. Crosby's donation helped the WOA to hire extra staff.

A crucial factor in the repeal of the Byrd Amendment was the ascendency of the presidency of Jimmy Carter. As a Baptist deacon and a born-again Christian himself, the Carter White House gave more access to religious leaders than any other executive in recent American history. It was also, to a large extent, pro-black Africa in its foreign policy. With pressure from both the Carter White House and anti-Byrd forces, it was not surprising that the amendment was repealed by an overwhelming number of votes in Congress.

The interest of the United Methodist Church in Rhodesia predates the enactment of the Byrd Amendment. No doubt, this interest was primarily based on the moral and humanitarian implications of the Rhodesian crisis. That the UMC has "partner churches" in Rhodesia with over 35,000 members, hundreds of schools, hospitals and other institutions only increased its concern with developments in the white minority-ruled country. Perhaps, no other factor influenced U.S. Methodism in its attitude toward Rhodesia more than the "Muzorewa factor." Bishop Abel Muzorewa, episcopal leader of the Rhodesia area of the United Methodist Church and President of the African National Council of Zimbabwe (ANC) was to the Methodists what Bishop Donal Lamont was to the Catholics, and perhaps much more. He had the potential to be to the UMC what Archbishop Desmond Tutu would become for Anglicans both in South Africa and all over the world. He is a graduate of Central Methodist College, Fayette, Missouri, and Scarritt College, Nashville, Tennessee.[260] He had important and impeccable connection in the U.S. Moreover, he was honored in absentia on the 25th anniversary of the Universal Declaration of Human Rights by U.N. Secretary General, Kurt Waldheim, as one of the "international champions of human rights."[261] Earlier in 1972, when Muzorewa had addressed a United Methodist general conference calling himself a "child of God in search of freedom," he drew a "standing ovation with his plea for justice in Rhodesia through non-violence, negotiation, and reason."[262]

It is understandable, therefore, that the UMC took a special interest in the Byrd Amendment from its enactment in 1971 to its repeal in 1977. Indeed the church's opposition to the illegal regime in Salisbury (now Harare) goes as far back as November 11, 1965, when the World Division (Woman's Division) of the United Methodist Church condemned the Unilateral Declaration of Independence by the Ian Smith regime. Commending the U.S. for supporting U.N. condemnation of the white minority regime, it reaffirmed its "earlier condemnation of the illegal assumption of power in Rhodesia by a minority."[263]   It urged the United States to encourage the United Kingdom

> to increase its economic measures against the illegal government of Rhodesia in order to hasten the day when constitutional government can be restored to Rhodesia under conditions that will ensure the prompt establishment of a democratic government with a new constitution arrived at with participation of all   sections of   the population, providing for majority rule and the improvement of the economic, social, and educational opportunities and conditions of the African majority.[264]

In a "Draft Resolution on Southern Rhodesia" issued in January 1967, the Methodist Board of Missions commended the mandatory sanctions voted by the U.N. Security Council December 16, 1966 and the application of mandatory sanctions by the United States...in accordance with the U.N. charter and the effort of the U.N. to restrict any economic activity which is not in the interest of the political, economic and social rights and interests of the people of Rhodesia/Zimbabwe. A good example of such activity was the importation of Rhodesian chrome into the U.S. with the enactment of the Byrd Amendment.

In all its declarations on Rhodesia/Zimbabwe, the moral and humanitarian nature of the United Methodist Church's interest is unmistakable. The church saw its mission in the light of the life and teachings of Jesus Christ: love of our neighbor and the quest for justice. According to the UMC, to be silent in fact of need, injustice and exploitation is to deny Him. With hundreds of churches, educational and health institutions and about 30,000 faithful in the country, the interest of the UMC in the Zimbabwean crisis is understandable.

The United Methodist Church, aware of her social responsibilities,

> has made a decision to stand visibly and symbolically poised on Capitol Hill to call the power brokers to accountability when the decision-making   process   threatens   the   viability   of   our   mother,   the earth,...menace the health and welfare of women, children and men; or endanger our continuing existence as human beings.[265]

In the struggle over the Byrd Amendment, two departments of the church played important roles. One was the Board of the Church and

Society, the other, the Board of Global Ministries. Based in Washington, D.C. and with a staff of forty (two of whom work in New York), it is mandated to

> project plans and programs that challenge members of the United Methodist Church to work through their own local churches, through ecumenical channels, and through society toward personal, social and civic righteousness...analyze issues confronting persons, local communities, the nation and the world [and] encourage christian lives of action that assist humankind to move toward a world of peace and justice...[266]

As stated earlier in the chapter, after the repeal of the Byrd Amendment in 1971, there was an effort to have it repealed from 1973 to 1974. The attempt failed. And, when success came on March 14, 1977, the United Methodist Church was part of it. Like other opponents of Byrd, it was not taken by surprise this time. Indeed before the repeal, the Board of Global Ministries and the Board of Church and Society had on several occasion called for such action with the support of the General Conference of the United Methodist Church.[267]

The UMC followed its official statements with practical action. In this, it had a potential advantage over other churches, with the exception of probably the Catholic Church. That advantage was centered on Abel Muzorewa, the Methodist bishop-politician, whom some of his admirers had hoped would lead his country to freedom through "non-violence." A regular presence at the church's General Conferences, Muzorewa was less of an asset and more of an embarrassment to the UMC by the time the Byrd amendment was repealed. By then, he had cast his lot with Ian Smith and lost the support of the progressive forces both in Rhodesia and the U.S. At a School of Christian Mission in the Western Pennsylvania Conference in 1979, Bishop Roy C. Nichols described Muzorewa's role in Rhodesia as mere "tokenism."[268] Muzorewa's attitude was out of touch with African nationalist aspirations in Rhodesia as well as the official policies of most American mainline churches. This deprived the U.M.C. of an important element in the ability of a church to exercise some influence on policy in the U.S. - the presence of a credible and charismatic leader, preferably a high-ranking clergyman, who is willing and able to explain to the American people the travails of his country. The problems of the UMC were not helped by the internal division in

Rhodesia between the followers of Muzorewa and Canaan Banana, another Methodist clergyman, who became president of Zimbabwe after independence.

For the UMC, serious action on the repeal legislation started at the conclusion of hearings in July 1971 and as the Congressmen met to "mark up" the bill. The chairman's task is to keep the committee moving, getting unanimous agreement on some sections of the bill, trying to resolve differences through compromise, and sensing when to delay or expedite matter.

> Because the chairman will likely be responsible for the bill on the floor and direct the debate, he or she will try throughout the mark up to gather as much support as possible. A sharp split among the committee members of the same party will seriously damage the chances for the bill on the floor.[269]

The premier method of lobbying was the telephone, a very effective instrument in emergencies. Four staff members of the Board of Church and Society were detailed to work on the repeal effort; but, they did not, however, work full-time. The staff of the Board of Global Ministries, who send missionaries to Africa, also participated in the pro-sanctions legislation. A "telephone tree" was developed and sent to the seventy-three annual Conferences that make up the ten million member UMC in the U.S. Specifically, phone calls were made to conference staff, board members of the annual Conference of the Board of Church and Society, and to the area bishops. Each of these had a list of church activists who were contacted and told to mobilize church members to contact their Congressmen in support of the repeal effort.

A more common method employed by the UMC was the use of the "directed mail." In its effort to repeal the Byrd Amendment, the UMC sent hundreds of letters to church members alerting them of the impending vote on the sanctions and its implications for a christian. The overall effect of the lobbying efforts of the United Methodist Church on the repeal of the Byrd Amendment will be discussed later.

CATHOLICS

In a series of statements and actions, U.S. Catholics showed their opposition to the white minority regimes in southern Africa in general and their support for the repeal of the Byrd Amendment in particular.

In April, 1971, the United States Catholic Conference (U.S.C.C.) issued its first important statement on the racist and colonial regimes in the region. Titled, "The Responsibility of U.S. Catholics and Racism in southern Africa," it called on Catholics to use their influence as stockholders in companies doing business in Rhodesia and other parts of the area, and to let "justice take precedent over profit."[270]   On September 23, 1976, the Executive Committee of the National Council of Catholic Bishops (NCCB) in its Statement on Rhodesia warned that

> U.S. corporations operating in Rhodesia... have a responsibility to evaluate their presence in more than economic terms, a moral responsibility exists to assess the role they play in sustaining systems which stand indicted and ostracized in the international community.[271]

Rhodesian Catholic bishops themselves were no less acerbic in their condemnation of the illegal Smith regime in Salisbury. In their Holy Year message, the bishops stated that the blame for the crisis in the country

> rests with the present Rhodesian administration and with those who support its racist policies. If there is to be any hope of permanent solutions, these policies must be radically changed...The real issues must be faced, discrimination based on race must be eliminated, equality of opportunity must be guaranteed.[272]

Drawing profusely from Catholic political thought, one of them, Bishop Donal Lamont had consistently called into question the political legitimacy of the white minority regime. He had also implied that the forces opposing the Smith regime had a moral right to the resources and ministry of the church in their struggle for justice. For his outspokenness, Bishop Lamont was expelled from Rhodesia only to return after Zimbabwe's independence.

U.S. Catholics also buttressed their progressive position on Rhodesia by practical action. In the Fall of 1973, Archbishop Joseph L. Bernadin, testifying on behalf of the U.S.C.C. at a Congressional hearing on U.N. sanctions against Rhodesia, stated that the

> current reexamination by the U.S. Congress of the U.N. sanctions of Rhodesia and relevant U.S. legislation involves two political issues which have serious moral implications. The first concerns human rights, and the second, international order. The purpose of this

> statement was to underscore the moral dimensions of these two issues raised by the Rhodesian question and to exhort the U.S. government to fulfill its moral obligations in this situation. The dominant moral theme that forms the basis of consideration here is that the international order is rooted in th inalienable rights and dignity of the human being.[273]

Urging the Congress to repeal the Byrd Amendment, he observed that the "U.S. violation of these sanctions·since 1971 has strengthened the position of the white ruling class in Rhodesia, has caused a serious loss in both the prestige and the credibility of the United Nations,"[274] and has damaged the efforts of all member nations to build a United Nations' structure that may, as Pope John XXIII earnestly prayed, "become ever more equal to the magnitude and nobility of its task."[275]

During the 95th Congress, more hearings were held in both the House and the Senate on the issues of Rhodesian sanctions. On February 9, 1977, Senator Dick Clark (D-Ia) opened the hearings before the Subcommittee on African Affairs of the Senate Committee on Foreign Relations by asking for the repeal of the Byrd Amendment, which the Senate had passed on September 23, 1971 to allow American companies to violate international sanctions.[276] Among those who testified for the overturn of Byrd was Mr. John J. Sheehan, Legislative Director of the United Steel Workers of America, accompanied by Robert Hayden, legislative representative of the same corporation. On February 24, 1977, Charles Diggs, chairman of the House Subcommittee on Africa and on International Organizations, presided over the House version of the hearings. One of the distinguished witnesses was Rev. Rollins Lambert, Adviser of African Affairs, Office of International Justice and Peace of the U.S. Catholic Conference, who reiterated the church's support of the repeal of the Byrd Amendment.[277] Such a repeal, he stated, would show the world that the U.S. supported the international effort to resolve the Rhodesian crisis, revealed its complete adherence to U.N. sanctions which would serve as a symbol to African nations that the U.S. supports human rights, disassociated itself completely from the Smith regime and make American policy more honest than the "verbal disclaimers which have marked U.S. - Africa policy in recent years."[278]

Another tactic used by the U.S.C.C. to influence American policy toward Salisbury was letter-writing. In an open-letter to the then Secretary of State Henry Kissinger on April 7, 1976, Bishop James S. Rausch, General Secretary of the U.S.C.C., reminded him that the "liberation movements are legitimate expressions of the peoples' desire for human rights as was the movement toward American independence two hundred years ago."[279] Urging Congress to repeal the Byrd amendment, he warned that the importation of Rhodesian chrome put the United States in violation of the economic sanctions against Rhodesia and, in the eyes of Africans, indicate insincerity in the statements our government may make about justice for black Rhodesians.[280]

In spite of all its efforts, there was, however, no concerted effort by the U.S.C.C. or other Catholic church groups to engage in full-scale letter-writing or telephone campaigns over the repeal of the Byrd Amendment. Aware of the church's limits, those Catholics who felt very strongly about the need to reverse U.S. policy toward Rhodesia sought other avenues to show their support. Most of them belonged to Catholic religious congregations and were particularly irked by the official church's weak opposition to U.S. policy. One of them was Rev. Ed Killackey, a Maryknoll activist, who in 1978 gave Rev. Ted Lockwood $5,000 in support of the anti-Byrd forces. Aware that his action would be misunderstood by some members of the Catholic hierarchy, he told the WOA director: "Please keep it secret. Don't list us."[281] Rev. Killackey's activism lends credence to the diversity within the Catholic church and the level on commitment of some of its clergy to justice and peace issues.

CONCLUDING COMMENT

The struggle over the repeal of the Byrd Amendment is part of the decolonization process in Rhodesia in particular and southern Africa in general. It is a struggle that has its roots in African nationalist resistance to British colonialism in the 19th century. That this resistance eventually brought independence to Zimbabwe in 1980 was to a large extent, due to the sacrifice and commitment of African nationalist guerrillas. It is doubtful that the West could have rushed to "save Ian Smith's neck" if there was not the fear that the African nationalists were on the verge of overrunning the country.

All the same, the contributions of international opponents of U.D.I. as well as the Byrd Amendment should not be discounted. These groups include the U.N., the OAU, the Non-Aligned Movements and many others. Crucial to the realization of African majority rule was the role of some churches in Zimbabwe and abroad. Within Zimbabwe, the Catholic Bishops Conference and its Justice and Peace Commission were outspoken opponents of the illegal regime in Salisbury and strong supporters of African independence. In their efforts, they received generous support form the U.S.C.C. and the Catholic Institute in London.

> The links forged between the Justice and Peace commission and the Catholic Institute in London brought events in Chriseshe Tribal Trust Land home to Whitehall, and the world, with a rapidity and accuracy that was acutely damaging to the image of the Rhodesian Front.[282]

Among Rhodesian church leaders, the premier prophet of change was, no doubt, Bishop Donal Lamont whose opposition to white minority rule and support for black majority rule was heard worldwide[283] and earned him arrest and exile.

Within the U.S., two churches in particular, the Catholic and Methodist churches, had the capability to influence public opinion as well as U.S. policy. The Rhodesian crisis presented an ideal condition for U.S. Catholic activism in more ways than one. First, African nationalist aspirations met the church's rationale for a just war: the reclamation of national territory seized by force. Second, it had the support of the U.N. and most of the international community. Third, it met the Vatican's principle of church intervention in other church's affairs: the knowledge and permission of the affected churches.

No doubt, the U.S.C.C. did express its solidarity with the Rhodesian Bishops' Catholic Conference not only in its statements but also by some practical action. However, there did not seem to have been any emotional commitment to the struggle of the black majority being brutalized by a white minority. There was no concerted effort by the church to use its potentially awesome network to educate and mobilize American Catholics in support of decolonization in Rhodesia as the church has done (and still does) over communism, abortion, and aid to parochial schools. Some critics of the church's attitude attribute it to its internal structure: the minuscule number of blacks within the hierarchy and among the sizeable Catholic population. The church's advocacy of "non-violence" hindered it from giving overt support to the African guerrillas.

Like the Catholics, the UMC was opposed to white minority rule and generally in support of black majority rule. Like Catholics, they also had their own "Bishop Lamont," Bishop Abel Muzorewa. However, unlike his fellow episcopus, Bishop Muzorewa was "a reed shaken by the wind." Pulled by the ideals of African nationalism and the realities of white minority dominance, he succumbed to the latter -

and lost. As the bible says: 'Since you are neither hot or cold, I will vomit you out of my mouth.'

Unlike Catholics, the UMC made a greater attempt to mobilize their members in order to facilitate the process of decolonization in Rhodesia. But they had their own problems as well. First, there was division among Rhodesian Methodists - between the followers of Muzorewa and Canaan Banana. This division also affected the U.S. church. Second, the dual roles of Muzorewa as bishop-politician was a source of anxiety to some church members in both Rhodesia and the U.S. This anxiety increased after Muzorewa threw in his lot with Ian Smith in the internal settlement.

There is no doubt that the churches have come a long way since the early days of European colonialism when they were viewed as the "advance troops of colonialism." Yet, there is something really wrong and troubling about a religion that is unable to fully identify itself with the dreams and aspirations of the majority of the people. It is both troubling and consoling to see African nationalist guerrillas, many of whom were baptized and educated in mission schools, seek and find solace and empowerment not in the traditional christian saints and symbols, but in the Nehanda of traditional African religion. It is troubling because it exposes the shallow and cosmetic nature of christianity as practiced by millions of Africans and its inability to inspire and empower them especially in times of crisis. The uninspiring nature of christianity in Africa was indicted by Ngugi Wa Thiog'o in The River Between:

> A religion that took no account of people's way of life, a religion that did not recognize spots of beauty and truth in their way of life, was useless. It would not satisfy. It would not be a living experience, a source of life and vitality. It would only maim the soul.

The dogged adherence of many Africans to certain beliefs and practices of the religion of their ancestors is consoling because it shows that in spite of centuries of colonization and evangelization, traditional African religion continues to have a major influence on the lives of the Africans. It was an influence that christianity could not muster in the life and death struggle to throw off the yoke of colonialism and white minority rule in Zimbabwe.

CHAPTER IV

THE REPEAL OF THE CLARK AMENDMENT

   This chapter examines the process for the repeal of the Clark Amendment. It is divided into the background, the enactment and repeal of the Clark Amendment, church group interests, foreign policy preferences and influence, and concluding comment. Its primary focus is the influence of American church groups on the repeal of the Clark Amendment, one of the most progressive pieces of legislation passed by Congress in support of the decolonization process in southern Africa. The struggle over the repeal of the Clark Amendment pitted progressive groups and individuals who saw the continued ban on U.S. military aid to Angola as facilitating genuine African nationalist aspirations in the region against conservative groups and individuals who saw it in racist and Cold War terms. Whereas, in the case of the

Byrd Amendment, a repeal forced the U.S. government to enforce U.N. sanctions against Rhodesia, the repeal of the Clark Amendment impeded the momentum of the liberation movement in southern Africa. It also increased the level of human suffering in Angola and promoted instability throughout the region. What factors brought about the repeal of the progressive amendment and its replacement with one of the most regressive bills on African decolonization ever passed by Congress? Where were American church groups when the Clark Amendment was being pummelled by its opponents?

> When first enacted, the Clark amendment was considered a great victory for those seeking to carve out a new post-Vietnam foreign policy along non-militaristic lines. To the right-wing, the Clark Amendment became a historical symbol of the dreaded Vietnam syndrome. Both concretely and historically, the repeal of the Clark Amendment and the renewal of aid to Savimbi represented the launching of a new age of global interventionism.[284]

BACKGROUND

Like most African countries, the history of Angola is characterized by centuries of foreign intervention. Motivated by the three "G's" - God, gold and glory - the Portuguese explorer-adventurer, Diogo Cao, landed in the Congo River estuary in 1483 to inaugurate several centuries of Portuguese colonialism in Angola.[285] Commissioned by his monarch, King Joao II, he made a return trip to Angola in 1485 to establish permanent relations with King Nzinga a Nkuwu, the Mani Kongo, or King of the Kongo Kingdom.

As usual, the Africans were initially hospitable to the European visitors. Soon, King Nzinga sent some of his people to Portugal to acquire Western education, signalling the dependency nature of the relationship.

On their own part, the Portuguese saw their mandate as a civilizing mission. In 1490, they sent their priests and skilled workers to evangelize and instruct the Angolans. The Mani Kongo was baptized, his capital rebuilt in stone, and his son sent to Portugal for studies.[286]

As usual, the cordial relations between the Angolans and Portuguese soured. It deteriorated after the enthronement of Afonsa I, the Portuguese-educated son of the late King Nzinga, because of two interrelated factors. The first was the Portuguese-inspired slave trade, which devastated the region and led to the export to Brazil and elsewhere of millions of people from Congo-Angola region from 1589 to 1836.[287] The second was the power struggle between white and mullatoe Catholic clergy to influence the policies of King Afonsa I. However, in spite of their differences, both groups undercut the King's authority and isolated him from his people whom he wanted to assimilate into the Portuguese culture of his training. The Portuguese clergy were well-aware of the danger posed to the colonial system by the assimilation of too many Africans into European culture: Assimilation, they feared, could lead to the demand for more rights, including even the right to a measure of self-determination.

From 1575, as the Portuguese seized more Angolan territory, moving up the Kwanza river into the Mbundu homeland, the first African nation to be subjected to European rule,[288] African resistance stiffened. This resistance took various forms: Syncretic religions, movements to restore indigenous kingdoms, ethnic-cultural and mutual aid societies, and literary, cultural, religious and youth organizations.[289] However, the ethnic sources of Angolan nationalism may be divided into three major streams: Luanda-Mbundu, Bakongo, and Ovimbundu.[290] And irrespective of their origins, aims and purposes, these three had strong religious underpinnings - African, Christian, or an admixture of both.

The Mbundu stream of Angolan nationalism may be traced to African reaction to the beheading of Ngola Ari II by the Portuguese in the 17th century, the exiling of his son, Dom Philip, to a Portuguese monastery, the destruction of his kingdom, and the elimination of all traces of Mbundu kingship around which future resistance would be built. However, some Mbundu did escape. Among them was a group led by a redoubtable woman known as Queen Nzinga Mbande (or Njinga Pande, 1582-1663). Having moved northeastward, she took over the new kingdom of Matamba by the Cambo River and tried to reconquer her kingdom. During a thirty-year war in which she never acknowledged Portuguese sovereignty over her nation, Queen Nzinga developed a "hardened corps of followers with strong religious element in their political association".[291] And even though her attempts to regain her kingdom ended in failure, her guile, resourcefulness and defiance made her one of Africa's foremost proto-nationalists.

The Luanda sub-stream of Angolan nationalism, which had a radical influence on the Angolan independence struggle, was a product of three groups: Africans (assimilados), mulattoes, and Europeans. For many centuries, the Portuguese employed the mulattoes, the offsprings of fleeting unions between white Portuguese and African women as soldiers, slave dealers and as sailors on the Sao Tome' ships carrying black ivory (slaves) to the Americas.

From the 17th century, the Portuguese used mulattoes to serve colonial interests, thus, sowing the seed of mistrust between them and Africans that had endured into the era of national politics.

All the same, the two groups cooperated in toppling the Portuguese colonial system and ushering in Angolan independence. While both often shared identical views initially, their approaches differed. The Africans were more likely to favor rebellion, the mollatoes, the press. From 1866 to 1923 - the time of the "free press" - many mullatoes emerged as champions of African freedom through their use of newspapers. One of them was Jose de Fontes Pereira (1823-1891), a symbol of protest and a pioneer advocate of independence for Africans in Angola. And even though they were often torn apart between two cultures, the main contribution of the mollatoes was the early injection of economic determinism and socialism into African nationalist politics. It was also this progressive attitude that led them to form the Partido Nacional Africano (African National Party - P.N.A.) in Lisbon in 1921, and to demand Angolan autonomy.[292] According to George Padmore, it was as a gesture to strengthen this group of African intellectuals in Lisbon who were then seeking political reforms in Portuguese African colonies, especially Angola, Sao Tome and Principe, that W.E.B. Dubois decided to hold the second session of PanAfrican Congress in that city in 1923.[293]

In the mid-1930's, other protest movements emerged. One of them known as Moise Noire, spread through the countryside with the message that African-Americans would come to liberate Africa from Portuguese oppression. Perhaps, the most important movement of the period was a group of syncretic religions made up of Catholics, Protestants, and African traditional religionists. Known as Kasonzola, it was banned by the Portuguese, went underground, only to re-emerge under one Antonio Mariano as a new prophet-protest movement called "Maria"[2943] Unconnected with the 'worship' of the Virgin Mary, the catechists of "Maria" preached a nationalist evangelism replete with incense, "Maria water", and praise for Lumumba.[4] The impact of this African religious protest movement would be felt in future Angolan resistance to Portuguese colonialism.

The end of the second World War saw the re-emergence of protest journalism through poetry and the Luanda literary review, Mensagem. Founded by the mullatoe Viriato Francesco Clememte da Cruz in 1948, and published under the auspices of Associacio Regional dos Naturais de Angola (Anangola), the Mensagem had as its slogan 'Vamos descobrir Angola' (discover your dignity or your Angolian identity). More importantly, it saw the black man's struggle in a global context, as portrayed in this poem by da Cruz:

Voices in all of America. Voices in all of Africa. Voices of all of the voices, in the proud voices of Langston, In the fine voices of Guillen...Generating, forming, announcing - The time of moisture. THE TIME OF MAN[3]

But in the maceques, the African slums around Luanda, another type of revolutionary poetry emerged. Contrasting the poor living conditions of Africans with the opulent lifestyles of whites and mullatoes, it blamed the latter for slavishly aping the Europeans and betraying their race.

However, the days of open protest politics were soon over. In 1950, the Mensagem and the da Cruz group were banned, eliminating all legal channels for protest. In 1952, about five-hundred Angolans sent a petition to the UN protesting the harsh colonial policies of the Portuguese government. Yet Portugal was admitted to the UN in December 1955.

Aware that old-style legal organizations and tactics would not succeed, a group of dedicated Angolan Marxists decided to create in the same year, a clandestine political organization of revolutionary character and oriented toward the interests of the popular masses and designed to gain independence by force.[295] The Partido Communista de Angola (P.C.A - The Angolan Communist Party), made up of Portuguese Marxists and mulattoe and African converts, was founded in October 1955.

In December 1956, the partido da Luta das Africanos de Angola (African Militant Party of Angola, PLUA) joined the Angolan Communist Party and other Angolan patriots to form the MPLA.[296] The manifesto of the MPLA called for the "overthrow of Portuguese rule and the establishment of an independent Angolan state governed by a democratic coalition of all the forces that fought Portuguese colonialism".[297]

The Portuguese crackdown which followed was facilitated by two factors. One was the Nove Estado (New State), a policy enunciated by the Salazar regime in 1950 to ban protests. The other was the infiltration of opposition groups by the Policia Internacional de Defensa de Estato (International Police for the Defense of the State -

P.I.D.E), the Portuguese secret police. On June 8, 1960, Agostinho Neto, an MPLA leader who became Angola's first president, was arrested, flogged before his family, and jailed because of his opposition to Portuguese colonialism. Neto, the son of a Methodist minister and former personal secretary to the American Methodist Bishop Ralph E. Dodge, studied medicine in Portugal on a Methodist church scholarship. He died of cancer in the 1980's. In response to the demonstrations that followed the incarceration of Neto and other Angolan nationalists, Portuguese soldiers went on the rampage, ravaging the villages of Bengo and Icalo from which their supporters came. According to Basil Davidson, whole villages were "totally destroyed with not a single soul (left) in them".[298]

The second stream of Angolan nationalism was Bakongo. Mostly rural and peasant, it was initially led by local kingdoms and traditional African authority. However, after Protestant Missionaries, such as the Baptist Missionary Society (B.M.S.), established themselves in the region in the 1870's, Bakongo opposition to Portuguese rule took on a christian hue. For example, in December 1913, a chief of the Madimba region, Tulante (Lieutenant) Alvaro Buta, a Catholic, led a national revolt against the Portuguese for their harsh recruitment practices. In response, the Portuguese not only arrested and jailed chief Avaro Buta (he died in prison), and his followers, they seized the opportunity to arrest Miguel Necca, a Baptist, and to burn down several Protestant institutions.[299] Traditionally, Portuguese colonial authorities who usually favored Catholic missionaries, saw the often more liberal Protestants as sympathetic to African nationalist aspirations and thus, a potential threat to the colonial system. In the early 1920's, as a religious prophetic movement in the Congo led by Simon Kimbangu (Kinbanguists) gained members among the Bakongo of North Angola, it posed a threat to Portuguese power - at least in its long-term impact. These converts came from two Bakongo exile groups: the Matadi and Leopoldville (Kinshasha). The clash between the Portuguese and the Bakongo exiles from Matadi arose out of a royal power struggle for the Bakongo throne. With death of the weak Dom Pedrdo VII on April 17, 1955, there was a call for a stronger king to represent African interests. The royal opposition, led by the multilinguist, Eduardo Pinock, has as its candidate for the throne one Manuel Kiditu, a Protestant and community leader. But the prospect of a Protestant king alarmed the Catholic clergy. Having quietly vetoed that choice, they supported the weaker Antonio Jose` da Gama, who became king. Not only were efforts by Pinock and his supporters to surround the king with Protestant advisers opposed by the Catholic clergy, their letters to Lisbon and the Vatican were to no avail.

Consequently, Pinock and the Matidi exiles decided to overthrow the king. On December 27, 1955, they mobilized a massive protest demonstration in front of the king's palace, where Pinock delivered a proclamation evicting Dom Antonio from the throne.[300] But after the Portuguese arrested its leaders, the revolt was suppressed.

Another important contributor to the Bakongo strand of Angolan nationalism was the Leopoldville group. With the suppression of political dissent in Angola, some Bakongo political activists fled to present-day Kinshasha, (then called Leopoldville) Zaire to reorganize their resistance to Portuguese rule. A prominent leader of this group was one Manuel Barros Necaca, a Portuguese-educated Angolan nationalist and former secretary to the late king Dom Pedro VII, who had earlier persuaded him to go to Kinshasha in March 1942 to organize the Bakongo. In 1949, recruitment efforts among Bakongo exiles in Kinshasha by Necaca and his young nephew, Holden Roberto,[301] failed as a result of the ban on political activities by the Belgian colonial administration in the Congo (Zaire).

Frustrated in their nationalistic aspirations, leaders of both the Matadi and Leopoldville groups sought increased cooperation with each other. In 1952, when the two groups approached the U.S. consulate in Luanda to present their grievances against the Portuguese, they received a sympathetic hearing. They were told that in order to gain international support, the Bakongo must place an able and independent-minded king on the throne. In 1955, some Bakongo leaders sent an unsigned petition to the UN demanding that Angola be placed under U.S. and UN Trusteeship. They also asked the U.S. to send a mission of inquiry to investigate conditions in Angola, especially given the Bakongo's fear of communist penetration of their country.[302]

The cooperation between the Matadi and Leopoldville groups was formalized in Kinshasha in July 1957, when their hardcore members formed the Uniao das Populaceos do Norte de Angola (UPNA - Union of the Poeples of Northern Angola). In November of the same year, the UPNA decided to send representatives to lobby for Angolan independence in Africa, the U.S. and at the UN. Through George Houser, executive director of the ACOA, Necaca was put in touch with George Padmore, Kwame Nkurumah's PanAfrican adviser, who wrote him in May 14, 1958 inviting the group to participate in the All

Africans Peoples' Conference in Accra in the same year.[303] In his place Necaca sent his protege, Holden Roberto, who met George Padmore, Kwame Nkurumah, and Sekou Toure during his visit to Ghana. He established relationships with young nationalists like Patrice Lumumba, Kenneth Kaunda, Tom Mboya, and Frantz Fanon. He was especially influenced by Fanon, the philosopher of the Algerian revolution who traced his Martiniquais lineage on his mother's side to Angola. Aided by the famous theorist of African nationalism, he finally realized that liberation without resort to armed violence was impossible. And most importantly, that progressive African countries like Ghana were willing to supply Angolan nationalists with the weapons to liberate their country. Nonetheless, Necaca also saw the need for supplementing armed struggle with a diplomatic offensive. Thus, in 1959, he obtained a Guinean passport in Conakry, and took Angola's case to the U.N. Through the A.C.O.A., he established a wide range of contacts in the U.S.

The Ovimbundus were not as influenced by Portuguese culture as the Luanda-Mbundus and the Bakongos. The most important source of change and influence were Protestant missionaries, such as the United Church of Christ and the United Church of Canada. By the 1800's, they had trained a cadre of christian leaders made up of teachers, pastors and nurses.

Ovimbundu kingdoms like Bailiundu and Huambo, which enjoyed almost total independence from Portuguese rule were not a real source of resistance to the colonial system. However, the insatiable appetite of the Portuguese for Angolan land and labor led to a general uprising in 1902. It was led by King Mutu-ya-Kevala, and subdued by Portugal in a major military campaign in 1904.

Ovimbundu opposition to Portuguese colonization has deep religious roots - Catholic, Protestant, and Syncretic. Its Catholic roots may be traced to 1950, when senior African students ("seminary nationalists") at the Christ the King Seminary in Huambo organized a program of general education in nearby villages near Luimbale. Instead of spending their holidays in the leisurely confines of the rural missions, they preferred to live among the villagers, and educated them on a broad range of issues - from the bible to personal hygiene to racial equality. Fearing that the seminarians were a threat to the colonial system, the Portuguese government forced them to stop their novel experiment. But before then, the students had engaged in overt anticolonial activities through the use of pro-independence literature and graffiti. Some of them were expelled. But backed by one German and two African seminary professors, the ex-seminarians joined others to form a secret society known as the Juventude Crista de Angola (J.C.A. young christians of Angola) in 1954. The group lasted only eight months before it was suppressed by the Portuguese authorities. However, under the inspiration of some of its former leaders like Joao Kalutheho, an ex-semiarian who left the seminary in protest during the mass exodus of 1954, new J.C.A. cells sprung up in other parts of the country, mainly Nosalisbon, Benguela, Lobito and the southern regions of the country.

Among the Ovimbundu, students from Protestant schools (student nationalists) played important roles in the promotion of Angolan nationalism in central and southern Angola. The vehicle was the grupo avante (vanguard group), a social-cultural club popular with Ovimbundu. One such group, the Organizacao Cultural dos Angolanos (Angolan Cultural Organization - O.C.A.), was formed in 1953. It was led by two Protestants, Julio Afonso and Jose Belo Chipenda. The son of an African pastor, Chipenda was educated at a Presbyterian seminary in Portugal, Hartford Seminary, Connecticut, and Pace College New York. In 1965, he was elected president of the exile Uniao Nacional dos Estudantes Angolanos (National Union of Angolan Students - UNEA), an apolitical organization which, nonetheless, distributed progressive literature from Portugal, Brazil and Ghana. On his part, Afonso was arrested by the PIDE while contacting two Ghanaian teachers during a conference in Luanda in 1957. Soon, the UNEA was banned in spite of its moderate position on Portuguese presence in Angola.

After Zaire became independent on June 30, 1960, expectations rose among Angolans across the border. As the anticipation of independence reached fever-pitch on November 14, 1960, the Portuguese authorities moved to counteract it by organizing a mass demonstration of loyal Africans as proof of the loyalty of most Angolans to the colonial system.

But some Protestant students at the mission school at Dondi refused to participate in the demonstration, in spite of threats of expulsion and worse. After the execution of their leader David Chambassuko, Angolan nationalists advocated a more militant political offensive against the Portuguese. One of them was an ex-student Julio Chinovola Cacunola and his supporters, who planned to begin a general insurrection on April 2, 1961.[304]

In 1961, three Africa-inspired upheavals occurred in Angola. The followers of "Maria" (Antonio Mariano) struck first, triggering a chain reaction of African armed resistance that shook the Portuguese colonial system to its foundation. Reacting to the oppressive Portuguese system of enforced cotton growing, in early January 1961, they destroyed farm tools, burned seeds and, singing militant hymns to Lumumba, Pinock, and Maria, launched a religious crusade for independence.[305] They destroyed barges at Cambo, Lui and Kwango river crossings, blocked roads, broke into stores and Catholic missions, and expelled the Europeans. Since Catanas (cutting tools) and canhangulos (hunting guns) were not used to attack people, Marianists considered it a pacific protest. As the attacks spread across the country, the Portuguese counterattacked. But as Portuguese planes and soldiers strafed and firebombed the freedom fighters, they ran into African ambushes. For several weeks, liberated African villages enjoyed a measure of independence. All the same, thousands of Africans were killed. Mr. Mariano and his main African ally Kula-Xing, were captured in Luanda, having been betrayed by two African traitors, who were bought over by the Portuguese. They were interrogated, mutilated and imprisoned. A few days later, when Maria's mother brought him food in prison, she was told not to bother anymore, "the customary if indirect way of informing relatives of friends of an African prisoner's death.[306]

The second attack started on February 4, 1961, when hundreds of Angolans wielding knives and clubs attacked Luanda's main prison to free political prisoners rumored to be transferred to Portugal. On the first day, fighting between Africans and Portuguese took the lives of seven Portuguese policemen and forty-seven Angolans. No prisoners were released. According to a Methodist missionary in Luanda, by February 10, 1961, three-hundred Portuguese had been killed.[307] Traditionally, this attack has often solely been credited to the MPLA, eventhough groups like the J.C.A. and U.P.A. probably participated.

The upheaval, which started on March 15, 1961, was in response to the Primavera incident of the previous day, when a Portuguese coffee plant manager, Sr. Reis shot and killed several Angolan conscript laborers, who were demanding six month overdue back pay. The revenge killing of Sr. Reis and his family by the angry workers led to immediate Portuguese reprisals that claimed about twenty thousand Angolan lives in "one of Europe's most barbaric suppressions of African people".[308]

Other than the shameful connection through slavery, the U.S. had no historic interests in Angola, an American tradition of "subsuming Angola under U.S. policy toward Portugal...".[309] This policy also included tacit American approval of the use of NATO weapons by Portugal to suppress nationalist aspirations in its African territories. U.S. support for Portugal became more explicit in May 1950, when president Eisenhower visited the country. Responding to prime minister, Dr. Salazar's request for and overt recognition of Portugal's stake in Africa, he praised Portugal's "contribution to civilization", and said that "we are united in a common cause".[310]

However, under the Kennedy administration, the U.S. broke with its Western allies for the first time, and voted with the Soviet Union in support of a Liberian UN resolution that called for "reform in Angola, progress toward independence, and a UN commission of inquiry into Angola". Disagreeing with Portugal's contention that Angola was a "domestic affair", and drawing from Jefferson's creed that governments derive their power from consent of the governed, Adlai Stevenson, the American ambassador to the U.N., told supporters of the Iberian country: "I regret to find myself in disagreement".[311] The New York Times called the administration's vote "... a new declaration of independence".[312] By April 1961, the National Security Council Special Group had authorized special covert funding for Angolan nationalist leader Holden Roberto to the tune of $6,000 a year. Robert Kennedy, the president's brother and the U.S. Attorney General, was the moving spirit behind this decision.[313]

Some of the churches reacted with horror and alarm at Portuguese barbarism. "In September, 1961, the Methodist Board of the United Methodist Church reported that in central Angola white civilians were attempting to decimate the male African population, especially those with any academic training."[314] As a reprisal, on July 28, 1961, the Portuguese arrested Methodist missionary Raymond E. Noah, imprisoned him for twenty-eight days, and then deported him..[315] By September, four other missionaries had been arrested and deported.[316] These Protestant missionaries were very harshly treated because of their pro-African nationalist sympathies. Perhaps in an attempt to defuse the crisis, Ralph Dodge, Central bishop for Angola, Mozambique and Rhodesia visited the country to survey the situation. After consultation with church authorities in New York, he attempted to return to Angola, but was refused admission by the Portuguese authorities.[317] Frustrated, the Board of Missions of the Methodist church documented Portuguese atrocities against the African population and submitted it to the U.N. The Board also condemned violence on "both sides," and attributed it to the "refusal of the Portuguese to grant self-determination"[318] to the Africans.

As stated in the introductory chapter, until recently, the Catholic church has traditionally been hamstrung in its ability to support the decolonization process in Africa, especially when it involved countries governed by Spain and Portugal with whom the Vatican has always enjoyed a special concordant relationship. Such a relationship included the exclusion of their colonies from the status of missionary countries, and were therefore outside the authority of Propaganda Fide, which oversees the church's foreign missions. Angola was such a colony. Thus, the unholy marriage of the Catholic hierarchy and the Portuguese colonial administration in Angola made it impossible for the former to challenge the status quo.

The attitude of the Portuguese hierarchy in Angola was not unlike that of one of their counterparts, Cardinal D. Teodosio, the former Archbishop of Maputo in Mozambique:

> Nobody can, in truth and based on facts, assert that Portugal has not nobly and humanely fulfilled her role as fatherland - Just consider the peace and order prevailing in the province during four centuries! And the social and cultural development, no doubt slow but real, which has driven natives from the jungle, bringing them into contact with Europeans and causing them to take an active part in social and agricultural life...Do not, therefore, allow yourself to indulge in fantasy or to be influenced by bad advisers, in dreams of independence or utopian economic or cultural happiness...[319]

And since Rome forbids sister churches to take positions contrary to those of the affected churches, the official American church was unable to lend her support to the deolonization process in Angola.

However, the Executive Commitee of the Au African Conference of Churches (AACC), representing millions of non-Catholic African christians, issued a statement at a meeting in Nairobi, Kenya, on September 25-26, 1973, in which it condemned the Vatican's collusion with Portugal and

> appeals to His Holiness Pope Paul VI to abrogate the 1940 Concordant and Missionary Agreement between the Holy See and the Republic of Portugal...appeals to the Holy See to use its influence upon Portugal to

ensure the abolition of the 1941 Missionary Statute...urges the (Catholic) Symposium of Episcopal Conferences in Africa and Madagascar (SECAM) to persuade the Vatican of the urgent necessity to liberate the Catholic church from the links by which she is bound to the colonial policies of Portugal in Africa, in order to enable the church to exercise her ministry of reconciliation between the African and Portuguese people...urges SECAM to take a position and lend its influence to the just struggle of the African peoples of Angola, Guinea-Bissau and Mozambique for human dignity, justice and freedom, urges the OAU...to call upon its member nations to review their diplomatic relations with the Holy See in light of its collaboration with Portuguese repression in Africa, calls upon member churches and associated councils to initiate discussion with the Catholic church in their respective countries aimed at joint action by all African Christians to remove the tremendous embarrassment caused to christianity in Africa by Portugal's claim that her colonial policies are in the interest of "christian civilization" and favored by bilateral pacts with the Holy See.[320]

In pre-colonial Africa, the Catholic church had usually adopted different strategies to deal with three different political situations. First, in cozy relationships with colonial powers like Spain and Portugal, the church deferred to the colonial authority, which really controlled the local church. Such was the case in Angola. Second, in Belgian and French colonies, where all the churches were regarded as equals, the Catholic church was more aggressive and assertive in demanding her rights and protecting her interests. Third, this assertiveness became more pronounced in British colonies where the Anglican church predominated.[321] It has been suggested that there was a secret accord between the Vatican and the British whereby the latter allowed missionaries into the country only if they promised to "steer clear of politics."[322] The racial views of both colonizer and evangelizer are similar. Lorene Fox has observed this trend in the relationship between Europeans and Africans.

You know, there is basically no difference between a white priest, a settler, a D.O., or a Police Inspector...They are all Europeans, and crossed the same Ocean when coming here. Don't you see how these priests discriminate against any African visitor who comes with a European? He is never allowed to enter their homes. Don't you all see how they refuse to give responsibility to the African teachers? If you quarrel with the African masters, you are punished. But quarrel with one of the whites, and you are sent away from school.[323]

However, as someone who lived under British colonialism and Irish Catholic evangelism in Nigeria, this writer did not see any concerted effort on the part of the Catholic church to promote the struggle toward independence. In fact, as a young mass server in pre-independent Nigeria, this writer never heard any missionary preach an anti-colonial sermon or in any way openly promote the nationalistic yearnings of the people.

While both the Vatican and the official U.S. Catholic church supported the status quo in Angola, other U.S. Catholics saw the need for change. One such group was the C.A.I.P. which called Portugal's colonial policy in Angola and Mozambique racist and against human rights, and urged "every American to end all forms of collaboration by the U.S. government and by private American organizations and individuals which give aid and comfort to injustice and evil throughout southern Africa."[324] But even though the position of C.A.I.P. was novel and progressive when compared to official church policy, it was obvious to Angolan nationalists that statements and declarations do not a fatherland reclaim nor a people liberate. By 1966, three nationalist movements, different in their social and ethnic support, ideological orientation, and foreign support, had emerged. They were the MPLA, the UNITA, and the FNLA. The three groups were to compete for power and primacy in a pre-independence Angola.

Several factors influenced the acceleration of the decolonization process in Angola. First, the OPEC - engineered oil hike followed by the 1973 Arab oil boycott exposed American political and economic vulnerabilities, and led to the inclusion of access to vital minerals as vital to U.S. interests. Second, the collapse of Portuguese colonialism, the rise of African liberation movements in Rhodesia, coupled with the Soweto uprising increased the demand for black liberation in southern Africa. Third, the victory of the Soviet-Cuban backed MPLA faction over their U.S.-China-South Africa-Backed FNLA and UNITA rivals drew southern Africa into the vortex of Cold War tensions and propelled it to a top position on the U.S. Foreign policy agenda.[325] Fourth, the recognition of the MPLA by the OAU gave it international legitimacy and led to its acceptance by other countries as the sole representatives of the Angola people. And, fifth, the forced reversal of the flawed assumptions of Kissinger's NSSM 39 by the passing of the Clark Amendment opened the way for a reexamination of U.S. policy toward Angola and southern Africa. The passage of the progressive amendment was made possible by the revelation of secret CIA involvement in Angola.

> When someone in the CIA leaked information disclosing the appropriations bill in which the CIA had hidden money to expand its dirty tricks, Congress overwhelmingly passed an amendment championed by Dick Clark to cut off their funds. Even Senator Helms was part of the 52 to 22 majority that cut off the CIA's money in December, 1975.[326]

"It is time," warned Congressman Robert Garmio, a supporter of the ban, "to state that we will not tolerate a situation where two or three men in the National Security Council or in the State Department or in the Pentagon, speaking in behalf of the President, initiate covert actions in a foreign country."[327]

Reactions from the White House and the State Department were predictable. President Ford condemned the Senate vote:

> The Senate decision to cut off additional funds for Angola is a deep tragedy for all countries whose security depends upon the U.S. Ultimately, it will profoundly affect the security of our country as well. How can the U.S., the greatest power in the world, take the position that the Soviet Union can operate with impunity many thousands of miles away with Cuban troops and massive amounts of military equipment, while we refuse any assistance to the majority of the local people who ask only for military equipment to defend themselves.[328]

During a speech to the Senate Foreign Relations Subcommittee on Africa on January 29, 1976, Kissinger stated the implications of Angola to American foreign policy:

> Angola represents the first time since the aftermath of the Second World War that the Soviets have moved militarily at long distances to impose a   regime of their choice. It is the first time that the U.S. has failed to respond to Soviet military moves outside their immediate orbit. And it is the first time that Congress has halted the executive's action while it was in the process of meeting this kind of threat.[329]

The Clark Amendment

In July 1976, Congress passed one of the most progressive amendments in support of the decolonization process in southern Africa. A product of the post-Vietnam syndrome in U.S. foreign policy, the Clark Amendment was included in the International Security Assistance and Arms Export Control Act of 1976. It states inter alia that

> no assistance of any kind may be provided for the purpose, or which would have the effect, of promoting or augmenting directly or indirectly, the capacity of any nation, group, organization, or individual to conduct military or paramilitary operations in Angola unless and until the Congress expressly authorizes such assistance by law enacted after the date of enactment of this section.[330]

Unlike the War Powers Act, which allows the Executive branch to intervene by political or economic covert means in a regional or national conflict, through the Clark Amendment, "Congress has defined as intervention, those actions which do not find U.S. troops directly engaged in battle, but do involve U.S. financial, logistical, and other support short of the actual use of combat troops."[331] It constitutes a straight forward prohibition of U.S. military or paramilitary intervention in Angola through U.S. assistance."[332] It does not, however, "forbid all forms of contact between U.S. representatives and other parties in Angola, it does not prevent the President from over-riding this provision of law and acting contrary to its stated intention..."[333]

As the State Department and the National Security Council were reviewing U.S. Angola policy in June/July 1975, the Senate Foreign Relations Subcommittee on African Affairs was holding a series of public hearings on southern Africa. The Angola hearings seemed so unimportant then that only one Senator, Dick Clark (D-Ia), the subcommittee's chairman, had the time and interest to attend.[334] Opposition from interest groups (apart from the executive branch) was not as strong as it was during the struggle over both the Byrd Amendment and the Comprehensive Anti-Apartheid Act of 1986. American business groups in Angola who would have traditionally opposed the amendment did not for various reasons. The Angola government had not nationalized or seized American firms; they had provided adequate security; had a viable private sector and were people the U.S. could do business with. Nathaniel Davis, the Assistant Secretary of State for African Affairs testified before the hearings that the U.S. was not secretly funnelling military aid to Angolan factions through Zaire.[335] But on November 5, 1975, behind the locked doors of the Senate chamber, William Colby, the CIA Director and Joseph

Sisco, the Undersecretary of State, admitted that the CIA was "covertly supplying the FNLA and UNITA with money, rifles, machine guns, mortars, vehicles, ammunition, and logistical support."[336] During a press conference in early December, Kissinger admitted for the first time that the U.S. was indirectly providing military aid to Angolan factions.[337] However, the cloak of secrecy surrounding U.S. intervention in Angola had fallen after Colby's and Sisco's testimony before the Foreign Relations Committee was leaked to both The New York Times, and The Washington Post.[338]

Thus, by early December 1975, the Senate Foreign Relations Committee had strongly endorsed Clark's amendment to the Foreign Assistance Act to cut off all covert aid to Angola. According to Gerald Bender,

the Committee firmly believed that the Angolan context indicated the U.S. could not win. Given the massive Cuban presence, an estimated $100 million in Soviet arms, and the poor quality of the FNLA/UNITA troops, it was concluded that the U.S. had no other choice than an immediate cessation of aid.[339]

With the cut-off of U.S. military aid to Angola, the MPLA government began to counteract the massive American propaganda against the young state. From February 25 to March 1, 1976, Luanda organized a seminar in Havana, Cuba. Among the twenty-six Americans who attended the unique gathering was Rev. Ted Lockwood, the director of WOA.[340] The nineteen U.S. organizations which took part represented church groups, coalitions supporting the MPLA, trade union representatives, and several left political organizations.[341] Six were members of the black press. During the seminar, the Angolan government complained that the Western press had created a monster as if the MPLA is a "red devil." The MPLA, it reiterated, is

a broad people's liberation movement, a front embracing people of various ideologies including Marxists, liberals, progressive church people and others." Proclaiming a policy of non-alignment, the MPLA vowed to prevent the establishment of military bases in Angola and the participation in any military bloc. However, it acknowledged that "if the Socialist camp had not helped us, our struggle would not have been possible. We pay a special tribute to the pages of heroism written in our history, with blood, by Cuba. We have been encouraged by the progressive trends in the United States to prevent further criminal adventures.[342]

In response to the request of the Angolan government, the U.S. delegation agreed to undertake <u>inter alia</u> the following program:
(1) Promote the recognition of the Angolan government by the U.S.
(2) Help dispel myths about the MPLA and the Angolan situation.
(3) Prevent a U.S. economic boycott of Angola.
(4) Facilitate visits by Angolans to the U.S. and of American citizens to Angola.
(5) Help to avert U.S. military aid to Zaire and to South Africa.[343]

As stated earlier, the Clark Amendment had several loopholes, which a willing president could exploit. After being initially promoted as a "Friend of Africa," Carter, increasingly influenced by Cold War calculations midway through his presidency, seemed inclined to tamper with the Clark Amendment. In his testimony before the Africa Subcommittee of the House International Relations Committee on May 25, 1978, Gerald J. Bender observed that both "President Carter and National Security Advisor, Zbigniew Brzezinski, are questioning if these restrictions are still applicable today against convert intervention in Angola."[344] Since the Clark Amendment restricts only covert aid to Angola, he stated, "any attempt by this Administration to repeal it is <u>ipso facto</u> an admission that it intends to undertake covert military actions against the Angolan government led by Dr. Agostinho Neto."[345] According to him, "Congress must exercise its responsibility to monitor and sanction the hard won powers over this important area of policy. Instead it is time to show once again the wisdom and courage displayed by members of Congress during the Angolan civil war."[346] Fortunately, Carter did not ask for the repeal of the Clark Amendment which would have led to the resumption of covert military aid to Angola.[347]

The Repeal of the Clark Amendment

Several attempts were made to repeal the Clark Amendment. On June 7, 1980, South African troops invaded Angola under the guise of a "hot pursuit" of SWAPO forces. In a move that may have encouraged Pretoria's expansionism, Jesse Helms offered an amendment on June 17, 1980 to the FY 1981 Foreign Aid Authorization Bill to repeal the Clark Amendment.[348] Since no other progressive Senator was available, Paul Tsongas (D-Ma) rose to counter Helms but ended up with a compromise that almost repealed the Clark Amendment. The

Helms-Tsongas Amendment stated that no assistance could be given to any group to conduct military or paramilitary operations in Angola unless the President "determines that such assistance should be furnished in the national security interests of the United States."[349] The president was obliged to describe the aid and the rationale for giving it (in classified form) to the House and Senate Foreign Relations Committee. The Carter administration announced that it "would not oppose the new Senate bill."[350] But a House-Senate conference rejected the bill and

> adopted alternative wording which technically repeals the Clark Amendment but substituted virtually the same prohibition on covert operations, retaining the Congressional authority over CIA actions in Angola. Under the new language, both the full Senate and House must vote affirmatively before military or paramilitary aid can be given to any group in Angola. The alternative language had been drawn up by several Washington lobbying groups including the Washington Office on Africa. Senator Paul Tsongas and Representative Stephen Solarz also fought to retain Congress' authority.[351]

The election of Ronald Reagan in 1980 ushered in a conservative era in U.S. southern Africa policy. Both the president and his Secretary of State, Alexander Haig supported the giving of military assistance to the pro-Western forces in Angola. Haig placed a high premium on ousting "Soviet proxies" from the Third World. He was also very critical of the Clark Amendment. "We found it too difficult...to provide a pittance of support to those who were fighting for independence and the values we cherish."[352] As a part of the 1982 Security Assistance Act, the Reagan administration again requested the repeal of the Clark Amendment. It also failed. But by late 1983 and early 1984, the administration was secretly breaking the progressive law. An October 10, 1983 Newsweek article on the CIA revealed that "training, arms, and financial assistance are given to the military forces in Angola."[353] A January 22, 1984 London Observer article claimed that "U.S. and South African envoys held "secret meetings" to discuss plans to supply arms to the Pretoria-backed UNITA in a joint effort to destabilize the Angolan government."[354]

Finally, on July 10, 1985, Congress repealed the Clark Amendment.[355] On August 8, 1985, Reagan signed it as Congress' first foreign aid bill sie nc1981. The House-Senate conference committee on this bill included the repeal of the Clark Amendment which "since

1976 had cut off U.S. overt or covert military aid to Angolan rebels,"[356] and a provision severely restricting aid to Mozambique. The bill had passed the Senate by voice vote on July 30, 1985, and the House on July 31, by a vote of 262 to 121.[357]

In reaction, the 21st Summit of the OAU warned that

> any American covert or overt involvement in the internal affairs of the People's Republic of Angola, directly or indirectly, will be considered a   hostile act against the OAU."[358] The organization also stated that "Mr. Savimbi is a known agent of South Africa, and has been responsible for the wanton killing of civilians, the destruction of the economic infrastructure of the country and the destabilization of the legitimate government of the   People's Republic of Angola.[359]

U.S. support for Savimbi, said Simbarashe Makoni, executive secretary of SADCC "is misdirected and very costly both for our region and for the people of Angola.   There will be no development, no stability, no western democracy, no free enterprise system to talk about. It will only result in further suffering for the poor people of Angola."[360] "Is it of greater American interest," he asked, "that we should keep (Angolan) peasants destitute and suffering in order to stop Soviet expansionism?"[361] But the State Department objects: "Support for the rebels," it maintains, "is intended to pressure the Angolan government to negotiate with them."   Given the deaths and the magnitude of human suffering, has not enough price been paid to bring about a negotiated settlement?

Proponents of the repeal of the Clark Amendment were, however, undaunted by these moral and humanitarian protestations.   After Congressional approval of covert U.S. aid to Angola, anti-communist proponents within Congress and the Reagan administration launched a massive campaign for the provision of American military assistance to UNITA.

On October 1, 1985, Congressman Claude Pepper (D-FL) (now deceased), who came from a district with a substantial right-wing Cuban-American population, introduced H.R.3472, which provided $27 million in so-called "humanitarian" aid to UNITA.[362] Motivated by their anti-'Castro psychosis,' Cuban-Americans, who seek to liberate Cuba were ironically promoting the cause of Jonas Savimbi, a man his former aides have called "another Idi Amin."[363]   On October 22 and November 12, two bills were introduced, HR3609 by Congressman Mark Siljander (R-MI), and HR3725 by congressman Bob Dornan (R-

CA). While the first bill sought the provision of $27 million in military assistance to UNITA, the second asked for over $46 million in military and "non-lethal" aid to Savimbi. In the Senate, Steven Symms (R-ID) and John East (R-NC) were also considering similar bills supportive of UNITA.[364]

As a result of the Congressional and Reagan administration push for aid to UNITA anti-apartheid forces· and their Congressional allies mobilized to counter this retrogressive effort to undermine southern African decolonization. On October 23, "six Democratic members of the House Subcommittee on Africa, under the leadership of its chairman, Howard Wolpe, began circulating a "Dear Colleague" letter to members of Congress urging opposition to aid to UNITA. That same day the 20-member Congressional Black Caucus issued a similar letter, citing such assistance as "wholly unacceptable" and constituting a "hostile intervention against the interests of Black people throughout southern Africa."[365]

Church Groups

Unlike the passage of the Byrd Amendment, the repeal of the Clark Amendment did not take American church groups by surprise. Ever since its passage in 1976, opponents of the amendment had slowly but surely been trying to have it overturned or, at least, watered down. As stated earlier, not even the "liberal" and "pro-African" Carter administration could resist this temptation.

Four reasons may be given for the lack of early and serious opposition to repeal of the Clark Amendment. First, political necessity compelled anti-apartheid activists and their allies, who are traditionally active on Angolan issues, to concentrate most of their attention on South Africa, which, at that time, was going through its worst crisis since Soweto. The subordination of the Angolan problem to that of South Africa underlies the importance of having an issue emerge at the right time if it is to get the right attention of interest groups seeking to influence foreign policy. According to Theodore Lowi,

> the most important aspect of the event is the time dimension. Is the event a crisis or is it not? Does the event allow time for consideration of alternative policies or time only for a conditional reflex? Are we on the brink of violence, civil or military, or are the events taking place at some point away from the brink where responses rather than reflexes, preventives rather than cures, may be appropriate?[366]

Second, the fervently anti-communist Reagan administration seemed to have been successful in convincing the majority of an ill-informed Congress of the need to aid UNITA and counter the Soviet-Cuban presence in Angola. Angola, therefore, is important in understanding Reagan's southern Africa policy because he saw the absence of an effective counter to Soviet-Cuban involvement there in 1975-1976 as representing a "major failure for the U.S. as a global power, with ominous implications for the expansion of Soviet power elsewhere."[367]

Third, given the chilly relations between the MPLA and some local Angolan churches, American church groups were initially reluctant to wade into the complex racial, ethnic and ideological maze of the Angolan crisis. For example, while UNITA is predominantly made up of "purely" black Ovimbundu, the MPLA, even though it is equally dominated by blacks, nevertheless, has a sizeable number of mestizos (mixed race) in its leadership. For institutional reasons, the UMC favored the MPLA, the UCC, Unita. The late Dr. Agostinho Neto, its leader and first president, was of mixed parentage and the son of a Methodist pastor.

The fourth reason may have been the most important. Since American involvement in Angola was covert, early Congressional actions were done "in camera" (secretly). Therefore, it was extremely difficult for churches or any other group to know what the U.S. government was doing. Ordinarily, in covert foreign policy issues, the president has a huge advantage vis-a-vis the Congress.

> The presidential advantage in foreign affairs derives not only from his near monopoly of information but also from the fact that on many issues in foreign affairs people have no preexisting opinions, a condition that no doubt results from a lack of knowledge or interest, or both.[368]

In covert operations like Angola, presidential control over information is overwhelming.

However, in spite of all the constraints characteristic of U.S. covert operations, U.S. Catholic and Protestant groups were involved in the attempts to repeal the Clark Amendment. Among these groups were the WOA, UCC, U.S.C.C., and Network.

Protestants

Right from the very beginning, the WOA was involved in the struggle to prohibit U.S. military involvement in the Angolan civil war. Its interest in the country was moral and humanitarian.

In early January 1975, Rebecca Schweitzer, the foreign policy expert for ten of the most liberal Congressmen on Capitol Hill, invited the WOA to brief the latter on Angola. Rev. Ted Lockwood, the then executive director of WOA, saw the invitation as an opportunity to enlighten the Congressmen on the Angolan crisis, and to steer them toward more progressive views on the issue. Present at the briefing were twelve Congressmen, seventy-five staff members, and Ed Mulcahey, the Assistant Secretary of State for African Affairs. In his twenty minute briefing, the WOA director stated that the U.S. should steer clear of the Angola civil war.[369] "Angola," he warned, "was a Third World strife and the U.S. has no vital interest in a tribal war."[370]

After the victory of the MPLA over its rivals, it was revealed to WOA through the office of Senator Dick Clark that the CIA was secretly sending arms to UNITA. This information was given to the WOA by Marian Albertson, Senator Clark's foreign affairs expert. The WOA director met her twice and spoke with her several times on the phone on the Angolan crisis.[371]

Seymour Hersch, the investigative reporter for the New York Times also visited WOA for information on Angola around the same time. Mr. Hersch had broken the story on CIA covert aid to the Angolan rebels in December 1975.[372] The WOA also addressed the Democratic Study Group on the need for U.S. non-intervention in Angola. In November 1975, Lockwood attended the African Studies Association meeting in San Francisco, where he circulated a resolution condemning American intervention in Angola. About six hundred people signed the resolution. An early January 1976 visit to the University of Florida in Gainseville provided the WOA the opportunity to raise people's consciousness on the Angolan civil war and the dangers of U.S. intervention.

In January 1976, the WOA organized a rally on the steps of the Capitol attended by about two-hundred people to protest U.S. policy in Angola. However, it did not have enough time to lobby Congress formally. Rather, using its three-thousand member mailing list, it sent out over four hundred legislative action alerts and bulletins to enlighten the citizenry of the moral and humanitarian implications of U.S. involvement in Angola.

From the enactment of the Clark Amendment in 1976, its opponents made several attempts to have it repealed, but they were unsuccessful until 1985. Like other groups, church proponents of the amendment did not seem to be serious and well-organized as the specter of its repeal loomed on the horizon. As stated earlier, they were like other anti-apartheid groups much more concerned with the deteriorating situation in South Africa. If their attitude was guided by an understanding of the geostrategic implications of a South African settlement, who should blame them for there is indeed the need to

> recognize that the fates of South Africa and its neighbors are strongly intertwined and thus cannot be addressed by separate policies. For Mozambique and Angola especially, there is little hope of stability, development, or accommodation with internal insurgencies until the threat of South African intervention ceases. That may be fully possible only when South Africa is pressed to resolve its own domestic political crisis.[373]

All the same, should not the need to protect Angola's sovereignty and minimize the human suffering in the country have been equally important to church groups and their allies?

Perhaps more than any other group, the WOA seemed to have understood the implications of the repeal of the Clark Amendment, not only for Angola per se but for the whole southern African region. On October 31 and November 1985, the "WOA helped coordinate two national press conferences bringing together several religious, trade union, human rights and anti-apartheid groups opposing UNITA."[374] The Congressional Black Caucus was one of the groups that took part on both occasions. Among the speakers at the press conferences were the late Congressman Ted Weiss (D-NY), Walter Fauntroy (D-DC), John Conyers (D-MI), Gretchen Eick, Rev. Jesse Jackson, Randall Robinson, Dr. Jean Sindab, Mickey Leland (D-TX), Catherine Broussea, Sister Mora Browne, Fr. Ted Hayden, and Martin Sovik.[375] Earlier (October 29), about fifty organizations belonging to the Washington-based southern Africa Working group had sent a letter to members of the House and Senate urging opposition to UNITA aid.[376]

The response of the WOA and its allies propelled Congressional opponents of UNITA aid into action. On November 1, Matthew McHugh (D-NY) of the House Permanent Select Committee on Intelligence and seven other Congressmen circulated a bi-partisan "Dear Colleague" letter urging their comrades to "co-sign an attached letter to President Reagan opposing aid to UNITA." This letter was co-signed by Congressmen Tony Coelho (D-CA), Julian Dixon (D-CA), Bill Gray (D-PA), Jim Leach (R-IA0, Stuart Mckinney (R-CT), Jim Olin (D-VA), and Buddy Roemer (D-LA).[377] On November 6, Congressmen Ted Weiss (D-NY) introduced HR3690, a bill "prohibiting any assistance, direct or indirect, from the United States to any groups fighting in Angola."[378] Anti-apartheid groups mobilized Congressional and constituency support for the bill, but it failed to pass.

The United Church of Christ (U.C.C.) was also one of the church groups that opposed the repeal of the Clark Amendment and the resumption of covert U.S. aid to UNITA. As the first U.S. Protestant church in Angola, where it has been for over a century,[379] it has a special interest in the country. Unfortunately, its partner churches in the country were then divided, with half joining the guerrillas and the other half cooperating with the government. Given its experience in Angola, the U.C.C. warned that "it is important that Congress decide the question of aiding UNITA with some awareness of Angolan dynamics and not as an issue of U.S. domestic politics."[380]

As the Reagan administration pressed ever-more resolutely for the repeal of the Clark Amendment in 1981, the U.C.C. issued action alerts in which it urged her members to write their Congressmen to retain the amendment. In 1983, the 13th synod of the U.C.C. adopted a resolution which inter alia stated that the

> United Church of Christ pursues the task of reconciliation in the following ways...declares its support for the U.S. government to pursue a policy in southern Africa which will be conducive to a peaceful resolution of the civil conflict in Angola that will respect the interests of all the Angolan people and will be conducive to a settlement in Namibia that will provide genuine independence from South Africa; urges U.S. government recognition of the MPLA government in Angola...opposes efforts by the U.S. government to provide covert or open assistance to any factions in the Angolan conflict.[381]

The resolutions of the U.C.C. against repeal did not, however, hide one reality: that the division within the partner churches had equally affected the American church, some of whom had UNITA sympathies. One of them said:

UNITA people are not devils. They have legitimate grievances." They
are also church-going people: "You did not ask about UNITA's relation
to the churches, but it too recognizes the strength of the christian
communities in Angola. Jamba has only four buildings of 'permanent
construction' i.e., not grass and reed: two wards of the central hospital
plus the Catholic and Protestant churches.[382]

In spite of their Marxist beliefs, the MPLA and the government had
also come to recognize the breadth and depth of the people's
commitment to their churches. This recognition was noted by
Lawrence Henderson, an American missionary to Angola.

A couple of recent signs of this recognition were the participation of
Lucio Lara in the 100th anniversary celebration of the Methodist
church in Angola in March 1985 and the presence of the Deputy-
Commissar of the Province of Sume (Novo Redondo) at the
celebration of the 10th anniversary of that Roman Catholic diocese.[383]

All the same, despite the division with the U.C.C., when Congress
gave into pressure from the Reagan administration in 1985 and allowed
the resumption of covert U.S. aid to UNITA, the U.C.C. was
unanimous in its opposition. Its support for the retention of the Clark
Amendment was not merely rhetorical, it was also practical. Before the
vote of repeal, the U.C.C. lobbied Congress strenuously. Gretchen
Eick, the church's foreign policy expert and the only one with a
background in African Studies, was their point person on the Angolan
crisis. She met relevant Congressmen and their staff several times and
urged them to help in maintaining the Clark Amendment. She
generated letters from church members in which the latter asked their
Congressmen to vote against repeal. She was invited by members of
Congress to explain the Angolan crisis to them. It was during one such
meeting that the U.C.C.'s credibility as a reputable source became
obvious. Gretchen Eick was addressing the staff of Senator Stephen
Cohen (D-CT) when she stated as a matter of fact that South African
troops had been occupying Cunene province in Angola for two years.
Surprised at her knowledge, Cohen's staff snapped: "You should not
know about it. It is classified information. Where did you get that
information?"[384] What the staff did not know was that the Canadian
branch of the church, which has a cooperative relationship with the
U.S. church, has a strong presence in Cunene province and supplied
the latter with the information! With this type of connection and

information, the U.C.C. made its presence felt on Capitol Hill on Angolan issues.

Catholics

The controversy surrounding the role of Catholics in the Angolan crisis is understandable: The Catholic church carries historical baggage in Angola. For over four hundred years, it was the official religion of the colonizer, the settler and the privileged. For an African to become a citizen of Portugal, he or she must, first of all, become a Catholic.

To a large extent, early statements from the Vatican about Africa spoke in generalities about decolonization. The Vatican, as was stated earlier, had concordats with Portugal. There was no specific condemnation of the ugly nature of Portuguese colonialism and white minority rule in Rhodesia, Namibia, or South Africa. Referring to Africa's racial problems in his letter, "To The Peoples of Africa, " on October 29, 1967, Pope Paul VI stated that "the aspirations of all men desiring to enjoy those rights which flow from their dignity as human persons are wholly legitimate."[385] He condemned racism as an impediment to the full development of the new African states and quoted Vatican Council documents calling it "contrary to God's intent."[386]

Unlike their Protestant counterparts, the statement of the Roman Catholic Bishops of Angola resembled that of the Vatican. It was generalistic and took no specific position on U.S. covert aid to UNITA. In February, 1984, the Catholic Bishops of Angola stated that

> our country is the victim of carnal hatred, with all the horrors that accompany it, dislocation of people, breakdown of families, hunger, sickness, death, and other evils of moral order. Even part of our country is occupied by foreign forces, in violent opposition to international law...Hunger has come to the point of menacing the people of Angola as it has done in the great epidemics of history...The war and hunger creates a climate of irresponsibility, lack of respect for life and the dignity of human kind. All those who are concerned about survival and dignity for our country will not hesitate to dedicate all of their energies so that the war will cease and the great Angolan family shall be reunited and reconciled. Angolans want peace for there is no other way open, either the extermination of the majority of the population or the Reconciliation of our severed country...[387]

While the reference to the fact that "even part of our country is occupied by foreign forces" obviously means the South Africans, no such nuance is even used either for U.S. aid to UNITA or the Soviet-Cuban presence in Angola. Perhaps, the likely oblique reference to American intervention is: "all those who are concerned about survival and dignity for our country will not hesitate to dedicate all their energies so that the war will cease."

However, two other American Catholic groups, the USCC and Network were blunt in their condemnation of Portuguese colonialism in Africa and of U.S. response to the Angolan crisis. In a release titled, "Statement on Portuguese Violations of Human Rights in Its African Territories" and dated March 19-20, 1974, the USCC-Committee for Social Development and World Peace recalled the resolution adopted by American Bishops on the 25th anniversary of the U.N. Universal Declaration of Human Rights in which they affirmed that "moral principles must be applied to foreign policy:" According to them,

> the pervasive presence of American power creates a responsibility of using that power in the service of human rights..The link between our economic assistance and regimes which blatantly violate basic human rights clearly is a question of conscience for our government and for each of us as citizens in a democracy.[388]

It states that "the numerous reports from Mozambique, Angola and Guinea Bissau provide distressing evidence not only of the violation of human rights, but also of U.S. complicity in these affairs."[389] The statement goes on to enumerate some of these violations: The suppression of African self-determination by Portugal, who maintains 150,000 troops in its African territories; in 1971, the documentation by the White Fathers (now called the Missionaries of Africa) and the Burgos missionaries of various massacres of the African people by Portuguese troops, in 1973, the testimony of Father Adrian Hastings, a British priest, before the U.N. of a series of massacres of Mozambicans by Portuguese troops. The USCC calls the

> link between the United States and Portugal...a question of conscience for Americans. We call upon the American people to demand that the United States reexamine its financial and military cooperation with Portugal...Finally, we again ask all concerned christians and church organizations to reexamine their financial investments in corporations

operating in southern Africa. Specifically, we urge them to associate with other christians in efforts to affect corporations' policies.[390]

Another Catholic group that opposed U.S. policy in Angola was Network. Network

> believes that the foreign policy of the U.S. should be based on the values of nonintervention, respect for the self-determination and sovereignty of other countries, peaceful negotiation of conflict, respect for human rights, and economic stability. These basic principles underlie Network's critique of U.S. foreign policy in Central America and southern Africa.[391]

On Angola per se, Network encouraged the U.S. to "employ diplomatic initiatives to strengthen and stabilize Angola so as to test that nation's stated resolve to remove Cuban and Soviet troops from its borders."[392] No reference, however, was made to Pretoria's campaign of destabilization in Angola and throughout southern Africa, even though the group is an avowed opponent of the apartheid system in South Africa.

Unlike the USCC, Network seeks neither the permission of the American hierarchy nor that of the hierarchy of the affected country before intervening in a particular case. It speaks out and opposes any U.S. policy that contradicts the values and mores espoused by the group. Angola was such a case.

Network launched into an all-out lobbying campaign against the repeal of the Clark Amendment only "after the cat was already out of the bag." Before then, the amendment was not very important to the organization. South Africa was. According to an official of Network, "Angola slipped through the cracks."[393]

Network views lobbying as the "art of establishing a relationship, especially with powerful Congressmen or staff who make or influence policy." Since, in politics, 'timing is everything,' Network used its relationship with Congressional staff to find out in advance bills that would be of interest to the organization in order to plot strategies for maximum impact on policy. But that seems not to have been the case with Angola. Nonetheless, as soon as it got involved in the struggle to restore the Clark Amendment, Network utilized the resources at its disposal. As Congress began appropriating funds that included covert aid to UNITA in May 1987, Network met with Congressional staff several times and once with a key Congressman. Using its 10,000 member mailing list and national network, it sent out action alerts three times; the alerts alerted members of the implications of U.S. aid to UNITA and of the need for them to express their opposition by contacting their Congressmen. The members also sent out over one hundred letters per month to their representatives in Washington. "Targeted phone alerts." that is, phone calls to leaning or undecided Congressmen, were intensified.

Before the vote on the restoration of the Clark Amendment, Network "confronted" some key members of Congress by the door of the Senate and House chambers and tried to change their votes. It was in this way that Network helped to change two votes in the House and kill the Iran-Contra aid bill. As a result of this vote, an angry White House staff member phoned Network and called Sister Catherine Pinkerton, the Network lobbyist primarily responsible for the vote, "Sister Pinko."[394] Congress, however has respect for Network because "they know you are not there to grease their palms but that you always come prepared from a moral and ethical perspective."[395] Another method used by Network to influence U.S. policy on Angola was the provision of "research results" on the country to Congressmen. The group, accompanied by Damu Smith of WOA, met Jim Slattery (D-KS) and provided him with their research on Angola. This helped the Congressman to develop his position on U.S covert aid to UNITA.

> Lobbying is, of course, much more than just quoting facts and figures to government officials and their staffers...Yet day in, day out, most of a lobbyist's job has to do with the sum and substance of issues. Profound knowledge of an issue is an advantage a lobbyist carries into battle. Other attributes can outweigh lack of superior expertise, but expertise can only help a lobbyist in his or her work.[396]

From January 1985 to October 1986 (i.e., during the 99th congress). Network made 38 House visits, sent one memo to the full House, three mailings to the field, two phone alerts to the fields, five targeted phone alerts, and one "sign-on."[397]

Concluding Comment

Of the three cases studied, Angola created more doubts and anxiety as to the true motives and intentions of many pro-African groups in the U.S., including the churches. In many ways, the Angolan crisis presented American church groups with a grand opportunity to exorcise several "demons" that have for so long possessed the U.S. foreign policy-making elite as well as the American public. The first is the "demon" of communism which according to Carter, 'paralyzes the people with fear.' The second is the "demon" of racism and white supremacy, which trivializes black achievement. The third is the "demon" of historical amnesia which would want Africans to forget the brutalities of colonialism, especially of the Portuguese brand.

In spite of the half-hearted and belated efforts made by American church groups to confront the Angolan crisis, even some of the most liberal and pro-African churches such as Network and U.C.C. nonetheless, nursed the "virus of anti-communism." Like virtually all U.S. administrations, they saw the presence of Soviet-backed Cuban troops in Angola as a destabilizing factor and contrary to the U.S. national interest as well as the churches' institutional interests. For both the U.S. and the churches, the ideology of marxism, espoused by the Luanda government, was seen as hostile and incompatible with their interests.

But these churches and U.S. policy makers seem to have ignored two important factors. First, that the OAU and other countries, except the U.S. and South Africa,[398] had recognized the MPLA government in Luanda as the legitimate representatives of the Angolan people; and that the Cuban presence was seen as stabilizing and acceptable. The second is that in spite of their socialist and Marxist rhetoric, MPLA leaders, like most African freedom fighters, were first and foremost nationalists, who, in the words of Olusegun Obasanjo, Nigeria's former Head of State, dared not throw out "one type of colonialism only to replace it with another."

Another "demon" which the churches and their allies could not banish was racism and white supremacy which influenced U.S. southern Africa policy. The attitude of U.S. policy makers toward southern Africa in general and Angola in particular is well-documented in the infamous NSSM39, which inter alia states that the "whites are here to stay and the only way that constructive change could come about is through them. There is no hope for the blacks to gain the political rights they seek through violence..."[399] This attitude is a product of the "Tarzan syndrome" in U.S. Africa policy whereby Africans are seen as harmless 'noble savages' incapable of fighting and dying for their country's freedom. This attitude was (is) shared by most Americans, including the churches. Consequently, when the MPLA came to power in Angola, their nationalist credentials were soon the country's tragedy as they have been on Rhodesia and South Africa. Perhaps, one of the reasons was the absence in Angola of a Tutu, a Lamont, or even a Muzorewa - a man with the skills to communicate his country's pain to an unwary America by his credibility as well as the sheer force of his personality. No doubt, Lutheran Bishop Curvalho, an MPLA militant, would not fit the bill either because of his ideological beliefs or other reasons.

A final "demon" American church groups could not banish was historical amnesia. It is a demon which still thrives in the life and consciousness of most Americans - black and white. It is the willingness to forget what is considered the uglier aspects of the country's history and to highlight the positive. For example, in recognizing the achievements of the Founding Fathers, most Americans rarely discuss their slave-holding past. How many Americans know or care to know that in the struggle for American independence, George Washington and his fellow freedom fighters hired the services of not only the French and other mercenaries, but of pirates. If the Americans could employ pirates, the Angolan people have at least, the right to seek help from the Cubans to defend their country. For, in the struggle for freedom, a new morality emerges, ideologies become irrelevant. All that seems to matter is the survival of the nation-state. This argument will, no doubt, be embraced by most Africans. It is, however, doubtful that American churches would have 'bought it.'

Surprisingly, it was the U.S.C.C., representing the traditionally anti-communist Catholic church, which seemed to have understood the African position - at least, by its statements. In his letter to Kissinger, Bishop Rausch, its General Secretary, warned that it

> would be a great mistake for us to view events in the African continent only in terms of a balance of power and influence against the U.S.S.R...One lesson seems clear from the African experience: even when African nations speak of adopting a socialistic economic system, they are not proclaiming loyalty to the U.S.S.R. or to the P.R.C. Still less are they desirous of becoming satellites or clients of these or any other nation. The record of failure of both the Russians and the Chinese in this regard serves as a warning that the United States, likewise, will not be able to dominate African nations.[400]

After describing African liberation movements as "legitimate expressions for the people's desire for human rights, as was the movement toward American independence two hundred years ago," he stated that "Americans should treat African nations primarily in terms of African objectives and African needs, not as appendages to the super power's struggle."[401]

All the same, that the U.S.C.C. did no more than issuing letters on the Angolan crisis is still baffling.   For indeed, the history of Portuguese colonialism is synonymous with the Catholic church's presence in that country.   Several reasons have been given for the church's attitude toward the Angolan crisis.   First, there were virtually no links between the Angolan and U.S. Catholic bishops.   And since the American bishops received no "signals" from their Angolan counterparts, as mandated by Vatican policy, they could not wade into the Angolan imbraglio.   According to an official of the U.S.C.C., politics within the church is a very delicate issue.   You are told: "This is the rule to play by."[402]

Second, on their own part, the Angolan bishops maintained a level of troubling neutrality.   Was it because they may have been at odds with the Marxist regime in Luanda, which, no doubt, saw them as heirs to and accomplices with a Portuguese colonial regime that had raped Angola for centuries?   Or was it because the bishops did not want to take sides so as not to fragment the national church, but to position themselves as impartial brokers in future peace negotiations between the contending parties?   Some of the sentiments were expressed by Lawrence Henderson, an Angola expert.

> The only sign of hope I see, and it is hardly visible, is that the church in Angola might attempt to mediate between the MPLA and UNITA. The Catholic church is the only national institution which functions in all parts of the country.   Individual Protestant denominations are strong regionally, but none has a large national constituency.   However, if their two councils - CAIE and AEA - could cooperate with the Conference of Catholic bishops, they might be able to initiate some negotiations.[403]

Indeed Angolan churches have recently played important roles in bringing about a negotiated settlement of the Angolan civil war.

What is, however, comforting about the Angolan crisis is that the U.S.C.C. did speak out on the issue with or without the permission of the local church.   But what is troubling - to paraphrase Martin Luther King, Jr. is not only where the bishops stood in times of controversy, but what they did in the struggle to repeal the Clark Amendment.   It is by the same barometer that the other American churches will also be judged.

CHAPTER V - THE COMPREHENSIVE ANTI-APARTHEID ACT (CAAA)

The primary aim of this chapter is to examine the influence of American church groups in the enactment of the Comprehensive Anti-Apartheid Act (CAAA) of 1986. An examination of the church's role in the passing of HR4868-PL99-440, as the sanctions bill was called, is important for several reasons. First, since the ideology of apartheid has a pseudo-Calvinist and econo-theological base, it is important to analyze the role played by American church groups in the struggle to overturn the corrupt and evil system. Second, unlike both the Byrd and Clark amendments, the CAAA was _sui generis_: While the two were amendments to other bills, the CAAA was a bill all by itself. It will therefore, be an important task to examine the impact of relevant church groups in the struggle over the passing of America's first comprehensive bill on African decolonization. Third, as citizens of the world's only military and economic super power, American church groups bear an extra responsibility in the anti-apartheid struggle. Their response to the sanctions bill not only sent a strong positive message to the global anti-apartheid movement, it was also a crucial determinant of a peaceful and non-violent transition to African majority rule in South Africa.

This chapter is divided into four parts: (1) Background, (2), enactment of the Anti-Apartheid Act, (3) the influence of church groups, and (4) concluding comment.

BACKGROUND

The Reagan administration came into power in 1981 determined to bring about "a fundamental change in the direction of American foreign policy as well as in domestic priorities."[404]   In foreign policy, it emphasized the importance of basing American interests "in realism, not naivete or self-delusion."[405]   For Reagan, political realism meant the rejection of the Vietnam Syndrome and the restoration of American military, economic, and psychological strength.[406]   It also meant the return to a rabid anti-communism that saw the Soviet Union as the source of most of the world's problems.   "Let us not delude ourselves," Reagan warned, "the Soviet Union underlies all the unrest that is going on. If they weren't engaged in this game of dominoes, there wouldn't be any hot spots in the world."[407]

While Carter initially tackled the problems of southern Africa with idealism and ended with realism, Reagan started with 'reckless realism' and ended with pragmatism.   For Reagan, the period of 'reckless realism' started with his inauguration and ended toward the conclusion of his second term[408] with the signing of an executive order imposing sanctions against South Africa.[409]   The period of pragmatism started with the imposition of sanctions against Pretoria and lasted until the end of the Reagan administration.

The first phase of the Reagan administration's southern Africa policy was heavily influenced by Chester Crocker, his Assistant Secretary of State for African Affairs, since it was the former Georgetown Professor who conceived and implemented it. Prior to his selection as Reagan's 'point man' in Africa, Crocker had sent out in a series of articles set out the guidelines for what he believed would be a 'realistic and successful' American policy as opposed to the idealistic and unsuccessful policy of the Carter administration toward Africa.[410]

On southern Africa, Crocker emphasized the importance of South Africa "as a focal point of the region, and as an actor whose ties should be strengthened with its neighbors."[411]   While condemning the Cuban presence in Angola as "totally anathema to American interests," he endorsed UNITA as "a major actor in southern Africa and one of whom the U.S. has to take into account."[412]   To encourage evolutionary as opposed to radical or evolutionary change, he proposed that the U.S. should "engage constructively" with moderate African leaders in order to remove or neutralize East bloc military presence in southern Africa.[413]   Thus, the policy of constructive engagement was born. However, while Crocker has been painted as an Africanist scholar, one can search his writings in vain for either sympathy or detailed knowledge of any part of the continent save white South Africa.[414]

Reagan also saw the white minority regime as a friend and ally. According to Kevin Danaher, "All he knows about South Africa is that he is on the side of the whites."[415] And he was, therefore, unprepared to abandon "a country that has stood by us in every war we've ever fought, a country that is strategically essential to the free world in its production of minerals we all must have and so forth."[416]

Thus, the first phase of the Reagan administration saw an increase in cooperation between Washington and Pretoria on virtually all fronts, "a serious retreat from official policy toward South Africa of the last two decades."[417] On the economic front, the U.S. became, for the first time, the premier exporter to, and importer from South Africa to the tune of about $4.2 billion.[418] This was a 24% increase from the preceding administration.[419] In November 1981, the Reagan administration supported a $1.1 billion credit facility to South Africa in spite of opposition from the Congressional Black Caucus.[420] From January 1981 through June 1982, U.S. bank loans to South Africa increased by 246% at a time when the apartheid regime was going through economic woes.[421]

On the military front, established U.S. policy prohibiting American contacts with the South African military was breached when five South African military officials, including the Chief of Military Intelligence, secretly visited the U.S. in March 1981 and met U.S. officials.[422] Moreover, Jeanne Kirkpatrick, Reagans's Ambassador to the U.N., also received South Africa's intelligence chief, General P.W. Van der Westhuizen, in New York.[423] In 1982, revised export restrictions led the U.S. to lift the ban on the sale of non-military equipment to the South African military and police,[424] and in spite of its opposition to the Nuclear Non Proliferation Treaty, the U.S., nonetheless, loosened its restrictions on nuclear-related exports to South Africa.[425]

But constructive engagement did not go unchallenged. Indeed, as early as the Spring of 1981, two "Congressmen of conscience," Stephen Solarz (D-NY) and William Gray (D-PA) had introduced two different bills to reverse Reagan's South African policy. These two bills would eventually evolve into the Comprehensive Anti-Apartheid Act of 1986. First introduced on April 2, 1981, HR3008, as the Solarz Bill was called, encouraged American companies to implement fair employment practices as advocated by the Sullivan principles. Inter alia, it required any United States person who controls a corporation, partnership, or other enterprise in South Africa in which more than twenty people are employed shall take the necessary steps to insure that, in operating such corporation, partnership, or enterprise, these principles relating to employment practices...are implemented.[426]

These principles include the prohibition of segregation of the races in any employment facility, equal employment for all employees, equal pay for all employees doing equal or comparable work, labor union recognition and fair labor practices.

The bill also prohibited any new loans by U.S. financial or lending institutions to the South African government or to South African corporations or entities owned or controlled by the South African government, the importation of South African kruggerrands or other South African gold coins, and the setting up of advisory councils in both the U.S. and South Africa to advise the U.S. Secretary of State on the implementation of the requirements of the bill.

Introduced on May 14, 1981, the more stringent Gray bill called for the ban of all new U.S. investment in South Africa since continued American investment "improved the ability of the South African regime to perfect its vicious and evil system." According to Gray, since only pressure could bring about real change, his proposed bill would both create such pressure as well as detach the U.S. from its immoral relations with the apartheid regime in Pretoria.

The Reagan administration rejected the moral underpinnings of both bills. Its opposition was allegedly based on what it called a recognition of the pragmatic realities of the southern Africa situation. The White House gave three reasons for opposing Solarz's bill. First, its restrictions would place American companies at a distinct competitive disadvantage vis-a-vis its foreign competitors. Second, its advocacy of divestment would hurt black voters. Third, it would extend U.S. extra-territorial jurisdiction by treating foreign corporations as American nationals on the basis of American ownership. Moreover, such a policy would, according to the administration, excite instant retaliation from the affected countries.

But the Gray-Solarz bills were not the only punitive measures introduced in Congress to signal growing American anger at, and intolerance of, the racist regime in South Africa. In September 29, 1982, Congressman Charles B. Rangel (D-NY) sponsored and introduced a bill that would ban the export to South Africa of American nuclear material, equipment, and technology."[427] According to Rangel, any U.S. support for the expansion of South Africa's nuclear capability would pose two problems. First, it would curtail the impact of international pressure on Pretoria and thereby hinder the struggle by the black majority for freedom and independence. Second, it would expose the illicit and immoral relationship between the Reagan administration and the minority regime in South Africa. "Is there not some basic ground floor level," Rangel wondered, "that this country is not prepared to sink below as it does business with another country that so openly violates the human rights of other people."

Another important anti-South African sanctions measure was initiated not by Congress but by a local government. In February 1983, the Washington, D.C. city government enacted into law a provision to 'prohibit' the investment of its funds in companies or institutions doing business in South Africa and Namibia. "In 1984, three states and twenty cities had similar laws restricting investments in companies that do business in South Africa."[428] Nonetheless, the action of the D.C. government was controversial, especially since it was technically under the federal government. Moreover, Washington was then controlled by perhaps the most pro South African U.S. administration in recent history. This administration saw the D.C. law as symptomatic of the growing influence of an increasingly well-organized and broadly-based U.S. anti-apartheid movement.

Understandably, the D.C. sanctions provision did not go unchallenged by the Reagan administration. Congressman Philip Crance (R-IL), an ally of the administration, introduced a resolution in Congress which challenged the D.C. sanctions provisions on two grounds. First, calling divestment, an important aspect of the D.C. measure, as "unworkable" and "ineffective," Mr. Crane's resolution claimed that sanctions would be counterproductive since it would fail to achieve its goal of a non-racial south Africa. Second, it called the D.C. sanctions bill "patently unconstitutional" since it was "clearly" contrary to the letter and spirit of the commerce clause of the U.S. Constitution , which gives the Federal government the power to regulate commerce between the U.S. and other countries. If states and localities are allowed to use economic leverage to influence other nations, Crane argued, "American foreign policy will become irrational and inconsistent."

On the other hand, supporters of the D.C. measure saw it as "both a moral tool to combat an immoral regime and as a form of pressure upon the South African government to effect change."

On February 25, 1983, the substance of what would become the 1986 bill was already taking shape. After adding segments of Gray's bill to his, Solarz and 62 other Congressmen co-sponsored a bill, which inter alia required all

> United States persons who conduct business or control enterprises in South Africa to comply with certain fair employment principles, prohibiting any new loans by United States financial or tending institutions to the South African government or to South African corporations or other entities owned or controlled by the South African government, and prohibiting the importation of South African krugerrands or other South African gold coins.[429]

Yet, it would take about three years before the sanctions bill was passed.

Three important factors facilitated the increasing clamor among Americans for comprehensive economic sanctions against South Africa. The first was the calculated and deliberate attacks mounted by Pretoria and its agents on churches both in South Africa and abroad and on other anti-apartheid groups. In September 1981, the South African Embassy in Berne, Switzerland, sent out copies of "Amsterdam to Nairobi: The World Council of Churches," a harsh attack on the international Protestant body by Ernest Lefever. The letter also carried a statement from Ronald Reagan insinuating that if the "World Council of Churches were also reasonable, they would not give any more money to the terrorists who kill civilians and missionaries."[430]   In the 1970's, the South African government used Muldergate, its $80 million secret propaganda effort, to influence world opinion and discredit its critics. One part of its 200 secret projects was devoted to churches, especially the W.C.C. The Dutch magazine, Elseviers, revealed the plan in several articles on Muldergate after, "Eschel Rhoodie, South African Secretary of Information and prime architect of the scheme, fled the country and talked freely to its editor."[431] According to the magazine: "The World Council of Churches is one of the most important international organizations in the world with which South Africa is continually at loggerheads.

In 1974, action groups within the Presbyterian and Methodist churches in America tried, on a large scale, buying shares of enterprises which had investment in South Africa. At the same time these groups began a campaign for the withdrawal of business investments in South Africa. In the American churches the idea began to gain ground that the faster a crisis develops in the South African economy, the faster a change of power would occur in favor of the Black population."[432] This caused alarm in some quarters.

In late 1982, the South African Embassy in Washington, D.C. sent thousands of copies of a Reader's Digest article titled, "Karl Marx or Jesus Christ" to U.S. church members. This article harshly attacked the W.C.C. Earlier, Pretoria, had created the Ecumenical Organization Bureau to counter W.C.C.'s anti-apartheid stance. Since it failed, it threw its support to the Church League of South Africa (CLSA), a rabidly anti-communist organization. The League was headed by then Methodist minister, Fred Shaw.

In 1978, Shaw and others, including Fr. Arthur Lewis, an Anglican missionary who was a Senator in Ian Smith's white minority regime, toured the U.S. The visit was sponsored by several people, such as Howard Ball, organizer of Campus Crusade for Christ and editor of the Good News magazine, Charles Keyser, United Methodist minister and key member of the conservative Good News organization, Major Edgar Bundy, head of the Church League of America, an anti N.C..C. organization, and Carl McIntyre of the anti-W.C.C. International Council of Churches. In spite of denials, the official South African Erasmus Commission which investigated the Muldergate scandal confirmed that some of these groups were secretly financed by the South African government.[433] The International Christian Network (ICN) was also established to counter the international support of the South African Council of Churches (SACC). Another group that attacked the churches was the Institute for Religion and Democracy (IRD). Founded in 1981, "the IRD has campaigned against the progressive foreign policy work of the mainline Protestant churches."[434]

Within South Africa itself, Pretoria's oppression of the churches continued. The notorious South African Security Police had detained and tortured christian ministers without trial for their opposition to apartheid. According to Dean Simon Farisari, of the Evangelical Lutheran Church of Venda, South Africa,

the torture you read about in the papers are just summary of what (takes) place...(A)ll in all I had to spend 106 days in (the) hospital because of these tortures. If a dean of the church, and a deputy bishop for that matter, can go through the mill in this fashion, how much worse are the things ordinary people suffer.[435]

The predominantly Black Roman Catholic Church has also increased its opposition to apartheid. "A recent pastoral letter from South Africa's Catholic bishops considered the proposed constitutional reforms" an affront to the people which ensures that racial discrimination will continue."[436] The oppressive actions of the South African government did not go unnoticed by the American people, especially the churches.

In early November 1984, the black trade union movement called the biggest strike in South Africa's history in which some three thousand workers closed down the Johannesburg area for two days only to be joined by four thousand students.[437] By 1985, civil unrest had spread to the Eastern Cape and other parts of South Africa. These activities provoked a cycle of crackdowns by South Africa's security forces that led to the death of about one thousand blacks by the end of the year.[438] A Business Week/Harris poll taken in January 1985, showed the 68% of the American people supported U.S. and Western pressures on South Africa.

The second factor was an event that happened on Thanksgiving Eve, when Congressman Fauntroy, delegate from the District of Columbia, Randall Robinson, the Executive Director of TransAfrica, and Dr. Mary Berry of the U.S. Civil Rights Commission, staged a sit-in at the South African Embassy and were arrested. This triggered off a series of demonstrations coordinated by the "Free South African Movement."[439] The demonstrators appealed to universities, churches and pension funds to "influence policy by selling their South Africa-related stock. In the following weeks, the arrest of more than twenty protesting members of Congress including one Senator, Lowell Weicker, Jr. (R-CN) and hundreds of other demonstrators including school children - helped turn South Africa into a public issue.

The third factor was the presence and eloquence of Archbishop Desmond Tutu, the charismatic South African anti-apartheid activist, who had recently won the Nobel Peace Prize and was in the U.S. to campaign for sanctions. As a religious leader, his presence and actions lent added clout and credibility to the moral argument consistently espoused by most American opponents of South Africa's racist policies. Presenting the perspective of the oppressed South African blacks, Tutu laid their plight squarely on the shoulders of the U.S. in general and the Reagan administration in particular. "Constructive engagement," he lamented, "has worsened our situation under apartheid, and has proved to be an unmitigated disaster for blacks."[440]

The United States, he declared, has "an extraordinary capacity sometimes for backing the wrong horse...We shall be free, and we will remember who helped us to be free. That is not a threat. It is just a statement of fact.[441] Finally, Tutu stated in unequivocal terms the moral roots of his anti-apartheid activism:

> We are talking about a moral issue. You are either for or against apartheid, and not by rhetoric. You are either in favor of evil or you are in favor of good. You are either on the side of the oppressed or on the side of the oppressor. You cannot be neutral. For failing to identify itself with the black struggle, Tutu told the West to "go to hell.[442]

By mid-1985, all of these factors had combined to force the U.S. Congress to take concrete action on the South African crisis. In December 1984, thirty-five House conservatives had written the South African ambassador, Bernardus Fourie, and threatened to support economic sanctions unless Pretoria moved to dismantle the apartheid system. In June 1985, the House overwhelmingly passed a bill (HR1460) imposing modest sanctions on South Africa.[443] The House bill imposed a ban on bank loans, new business investment and the importation of kruggerrands. In July, the Senate passed an even more modest bill banning bank loans and the export of nuclear and computer technology to South Africa. On July 31, 1985, a House-Senate conference approved the imposition of a ban on South African kruggerrands.

However, perhaps the most unexpected reversal of policy took place at the White House. In a bid to steal Congress' thunder, Reagan, in September 1985, introduced an executive order which, among other things, included: a ban on computer exports, a prohibition on all exports of nuclear goods and technology, and a ban on loans to the government, except on humanitarian or social grounds.[444] Reagan's maneuver almost succeeded. For it prompted two leading Republican Senators to initiate a successful filibuster of the conference bill. In fact, in order to "ensure the bill's death, Dole and Lugar took the official copy from the Senate chamber and locked it in the Foreign Relations Committee safe."[445]

But the sanctions juggernaut in Congress could not be stopped because of two important developments within and outside of South Africa. In June 1986, Pretoria, anticipating demonstrations marking the 1976 Soweto riots, imposed strict press censorship and a sweeping state of emergency. On January 13, 1986, 120 U.S. church leaders, representing 25 denominations (Orthodox, Protestant, and Roman Catholic) met in Washington, D.C. to establish a "Churches Emergency Committee on southern Africa."[446] The gathering was in response to a December 1985 meeting in Harare, Zimbabwe, when church leaders from around the world held discussions with a delegation of 45 South African church leaders on how the global religious community could be of assistance in the fights against apartheid. Galvanized by the publication of the Kairos Document in September 1985, South African church leaders asked the W.C.C. to discuss strategies for ending apartheid. The Kairos Document states inter alia - that the church cannot collaborate with tyranny neither can it do anything that appears to give legitimacy to a morally illegitimate regime unless to submerge itself in the escalating liberation struggle, to reject reformist notions of justice in South Africa, to create special church programs to aid the struggle and to call for the replacement of the present government.

From December 4-6, the church leaders met in Harare, Zimbabwe and adopted the Harare Declaration, a passionate plea or f action aimed particularly at the churches of the U.S. and Europe. Among other things, the Declaration issued the first unequivocal call by the international church representative for the resignation of the South African government as "the most appropriate and least costly process of change" in South Africa. It also called on the churches to support South African movements working for the liberation of their country as well as the W.C.C.'s Program to Combat Racism. Among the church leaders present in Harare were Rev. Avery Post of the U.C.C., Bishop James Aulk of the U.M.C., Dr. Lorenzo Shepard of the Progressive National Baptist Convention and delegates from three other historically Black denominations: African Methodist Episcopal, African Methodist Episcopal-Zion, and Christian Methodist Episcopal.[447]

With the establishment of the Churches Emergency Committee on southern Africa, American churches intensified their anti-apartheid campaigns. They utilized the NCC's Africa office's "South Africa: Agenda 1986" as a program to conduct educational campaigns in the churches, sustain lobbying efforts in Congress and raise funds for South African refugees and victims of apartheid within South Africa. For them, as it was for the churches in South Africa, the moment of "kairos" (time of truth) had arrived: the churches were moving beyond prayers and appeals to conscience to intensify outright divestment of their funds from companies doing business in South Africa.

THE ENACTMENT OF THE CAAA

The House was the first to react to the draconian measures of the South African government. In response to Pretoria's crackdown, the House took up HR 4868, a bill which strengthened Reagan's executive order. It, however, added new sanctions measures, such as the prohibition of new business investments in South Africa. In a gamble that proved to be costly to opponents of congressional sanctions, House Republicans allowed a "radical" amendment sponsored by Ronald V. Dellums (D-CA) to pass without a challenge, hoping that its passage in the House would certainly doom any sanctions compromise with the Senate. But, they miscalculated. For instead of derailing the sanctions bill, the Dellum's amendment, which had called for the suspension of all trade with South Africa and the forcing of U.S. businesses to leave the country within six months, "shifted the entire political balance on South Africa, establishing a new set of limits for what Congress could consider and making any other set of sanctions seem moderate by comparison."[448] A July 22, 1986 nationally televised speech by Reagan on the eve of the Senate Foreign Relations Committee hearings on South Africa failed to quell the clamor for sanctions in the Senate.

A key player in the pro-sanctions group in the Senate was Lugar, a former Reagan ally who, together with Nancy Landon Kassebaum (R-KS) had urged Reagan to embrace a tougher anti-apartheid position. But having failed to change substantially the President's attitude toward Pretoria, Lugar introduced his own more moderate bill, which included several export bans and a prohibition on new business investment in South Africa. After the Senate passed his sanctions bill 84-14 on August 15, Lugar was able to convince the House to bypass a conference committee and to accept the Senate version. On September 12, 1986, the House sent the Senate bill to Reagan by a 308-77 vote.[449] On September 26, Reagan vetoed the bill claiming it would impose "sweeping punitive sanctions that would injure most the very people we seek to help."[450]

Congressional response to Reagan veto was immediate and historic. On September 29, the House acted to override his veto by a margin of 313 to 83. On October 2, 1986, the Senate overrode Reagan's veto by a vote of 78-21 and passed the Comprehensive Anti-Apartheid Act of 1986.[451] This marked the third time in recent American history that Congress has overridden a Presidential veto on a major foreign policy issue.[452] The override "marked the most serious defeat Reagan had suffered on a foreign policy issue and one of the stunning blows of his

Presidency."[453] The Anti-Apartheid Act of 1986 <u>inter alia</u> banned all U.S. import of South African iron, steel, coal, uranium, textiles, agricultural products and the sale of kruggerrands. It also banned new loans and investment in South Africa and forbade South African airways from landing in the U.S.[454]

CHURCH GROUPS

Some of the those who are ill-informed about the churches' role in South Africa have often accused them of either being soft on the apartheid system or of outright complicity with Pretoria, or both. That is far from the truth. Within South Africa itself, with the exception of the Nederduitse Gereformeerde Kerk (N.G.K. or the South African Dutch Reformed Church) to which most Afrikaners belong[455] and the Nederduitsch Hervormde (NHK), most churches have for many years been opposed to the racist policies of the South African government. Even within the Dutch Reformed church, it was not until the 1857 Synod that the church declared that the "Heathen" must "enjoy christian privileges" in separate buildings if whites objected to having communion with them."[456] This statement was a reversal of an 1829 pronouncement which declared that the Word of God called for communion to be served to all members "without distinction of color or origin."[457]

In the U.S., according to Deats, "attitudinal differences among Catholic, Protestant, and Jewish religious constituencies regarding South Africa and U.S. policy with respect to it are minor to insignificant."[458] There is equally "a remarkable consensus among church leaders for change in South Africa."[459] In spite of this consensus, however, the historical roles of U.S. Catholic and Protestant groups in the shaping of American policy toward Pretoria also influenced their attitudes during the struggle over the enactment of the CAAA. The churches' extraordinary interest in South Africa is propelled by the fact that "although apartheid refers primarily to the policy of the National Party government in South Africa,...that policy has theological and ecclesiastical roots as well as powerful social-ethical and ecclesiological effects."[460] The U.S.C.C. and Network were among Catholic groups involved in the passage of the CAAA: Among the Protestants, the Episcopal Church, and the United Church of Christ were active.

CATHOLICS

As a church operating in a traditionally anti-Catholic and Afrikaner-dominated society, the South African Catholic church has, nonetheless, been sensitive to the racial problems of South Africa. Although it was not as activist as some would have preferred until recently the church has for several decades, and on several occasions, spoken out against the apartheid system. In pastoral letters dating back to a "Statement on Race Relations" in 1952, the southern African Bishops' Conference (SABC) has often "called for reforms in South Africa and an end to racial discrimination."[461] In a 1957 "Statement on Apartheid," the Catholic hierarchy, for the first time, referred to apartheid as "intrinsically evil."[462] They restated their opposition to apartheid in 1962 by observing that "as christian people we dare not remain silent and passive in face of the injustices inflicted on members of the unprivileged racial groups."[463]

In the 1970's, church opposition intensified with the publication of several statements condemning Pretoria's denial of human rights to the majority of its citizens. These included "A Statement on the Restriction of Civil Liberties," "A Call to Conscience by the Bishops," "Statement on Detentions and Bannings," "Statement on the 1976 Unrest," and a "Statement on the Current Situation and Citizen Rights of Blacks." A "Declaration of Commitment on Social Justice and Race Relations Within the Church," published in 1977, challenged apartheid (as required by law) within the church itself. Having desegregated their schools one year earlier, the bishops summed up the situation in the country by stating that black people in South Africa have "passed the point of no return." In 1978, the bishops defended the right to mixed worship and sent a letter to the Prime Minister protesting arrests and detentions of anti-apartheid activists. In 1979, they repudiated the actions of the South African Catholic Defense League which equates concern for social justice with communism or Marxism.

In 1984, the SABC collaborated with the South African Council of Churches in publishing an important document titled, "Relocations: The Churches' Report on Forced Removals in South Africa." The document condemned the forced removals of blacks from their homes as leading to "a worsening of social and economic conditions." Calling their action a "decision of conscience" and "a Gethsemane experience," the SABC on May 2, 1986 endorsed economic pressures against the apartheid regime. They took this stand by filing shareholder resolutions with portfolio corporations doing business in South Africa, requiring them to implement a disinvestment program by withdrawal from South Africa." On May 15, 1987, an ad hoc committee of bishops appointed to monitor any improvement in the apartheid system, not only reported a negative outcome but went out of its way to warn that "the situation is likely to deteriorate further."[464] The acceptance of the committee's report by the U.S.C.C. Executive Committee led to the completion of divestment by the U.S.C.C., a process which started with the release of the September 10, 1986 policy statement.

On the local level, the Archdiocese of Baltimore was "the first Roman Catholic diocese to divest itself of all holdings in companies that do business with South Africa."[465] Given its history of social activism, especially under Archbishop Borders and his black Auxiliary, Bishop John Ricard, "South African-related investments were targeted for divestment first because of the critical human rights situation in that country."[466]

On sanctions against South Africa, however, the U.S.C.C.'s position was somewhat ambiguous. They may have been hampered from giving full support to sanctions by the Vatican's directive that the various national churches coordinate their activities on foreign policy issues. In spite of their vehement opposition to apartheid in their own country, the South African Catholic Bishops Conference (SACBC) has resisted the imposition of sanctions on Pretoria for years. Their opposition was based on the belief that sanctions would bring increased hardship to those who were already suffering the effects of "the unprecedented seriousness of our present crisis, the enormity of the present suffering of the oppressed people of South Africa and the horrifying specter of escalating violence."[467] A commission was set up to monitor the adverse effects of sanctions on blacks.

For their own part, American Catholic groups were no less condemnatory in their statements and actions on South Africa. In March 1971, the Committee for International Affairs of the U.S.C.C. issued a statement entitled, "The Responsibility of U.S. Catholics and Racism in southern Africa." The statement called on Catholics stockholders in companies doing business in South Africa to "use their influence" to bring about change in that troubled country. From 1975 to 1985, the church issued statements critical of both apartheid and U.S. policy. These include Bishop James Rausch's (General Secretary of the U.S.C.C.) "Statement On the United Nations and the Republic of South Africa, (1975) and "Letter to Kissinger on southern Africa (1976)," U.S.C.C.'s "Southern Africa: Peace or War," (1976) and Rev. J. Bryan Hehir's (Associate Secretary, U.S.C.C.) "Letter to Transportation Secretary Brock Adams."

Declaring that "apartheid stands as a contradiction to the basic christian teaching on human dignity and the human person," the U.S.C.C. Administrative Board issued its "Statement on South Africa" on September 11, 1985 and "endorsed the Anti-Apartheid Action Act of 1985."[468] On September 10, 1986, the U.S. Catholic Bishops issued "Divestment, Disinvestment, and South Africa" in which they demanded that the South African government begin dismantling the system of apartheid and to engage in serious negotiations with legitimate black leaders by May 15, 1987,"[469] or they would call on dioceses and church-related institutions to "consider the prudent and fiscally responsible divestment from business in South Africa or to begin to file, encourage, and join with others in most blacks.

But their position contradicted that of most black South Africans as well as anti-apartheid groups world-wide. Asked about sanctions, most black South African opponent of apartheid often quote chief Albert Luthuli:

> Economic boycott of South Africa will entail undoubted hardships for Africans. We do not doubt that. But, if it is a method which shortens the day of bloodshed, the suffering to us will be a price we are willing to pay. In any case, we suffer already, our children are often undernourished, and on a small scale, so far, we die at the whim of a policeman.[470]

After initial hesitation, Tutu also approved of sanctions: Our country is burning and bleeding, he lamented, so I call on the international community to apply punitive sanctions against this government to help us establish a new South Africa nonracial, democratic, participatory and just.

Given the clear and majority black South African support for sanctions, the continued opposition by the SACBC and USCC seemed untenable and paternalistic. And even after the U.S. and other countries had imposed economic sanctions against Pretoria, the SACBC and the USCC were still hesitant. On May 11, 1987, Bishop Wilfred Napier of Kokstad, president of the SACBC issued a statement on economic sanctions:

> it is too early to predict the outcome of the imposition of sanctions, and the effect that they are having either on the employment position or on white opinion...Many blacks appear to be consolidating their resolve to cope with the results of any economic pressures that may be brought

against this country...Much of so-called big business and vested interests continue to support the government and its policies to exclude black people from any meaningful participation in the decision making process, whether actively or by silence complicity.[471]

Earlier, on May 2, 1986, the SACBC, after characterizing apartheid as "something intrinsically evil," issued a statement which inter alia said: "We ourselves believe that economic pressure has been justifiably imposed to end apartheid. Moreover, we believe that such pressure should continue and, if necessary, be intensified should...developments...show little hope of fundamental change."[472] While this statement advocates "economic pressure," should it be taken as a sign of outright support for "economic sanctions" by the Catholic bishops of South Africa? This may not have been the case because the bishops' pastoral letter did not contain the "S" word (ie sanctions). It was not even a total but merely "qualified support to economic 'pressures' aimed at ending apartheid."[473]

American Catholic Bishops have two direct ties to South Africa. "First, bonds of episcopal solidarity make the Catholic Church one of a handful of institutions that can act in a coordinated way in both countries. Second, the members of the Church in the United States are citizens of a country with a significant impact on South Africa."[474] Ordinarily, these bonds as well as traditional church practice would have the U.S. church await "signals" from the South African church before making important policy statements on the troubled country. But this seems not to have been the case on this issue. Thus, on the question of sanctions, there seems to be a contradiction between the official statements of the American Catholic Bishops and those of the staff of the U.S.C.C. On November 15, 1984, during a meeting of the NCCB, seventeen U.S. Catholic Bishops issued a statement which called for "an end to the Reagan administration's policy of constructive engagement toward South Africa."[475] They called apartheid a system which is "evil, diabolical, and must be eliminated."[476] Calling for "an unambiguous U.S. policy of commitment to human rights in South Africa," the U.S.C.C. Administrative Board on September 11, 1985, called for the "approval of the Anti-Apartheid Action Act of 1985, now pending before the Congress."[477] In a letter to the Senate Foreign Relations Committee, Monsignor Daniel F. Hoye, General Secretary of the U.S.C.C., indicated that his organization had supported comprehensive sanctions against Pretoria: "While the limited sanctions imposed by the Executive Order of September 9,1985 and the more inclusive ones mandated by the Legislation of October 2, 1986, which we supported, had relatively little economic impact, they sent an important political signal which had significant impact in South Africa."[478] Since by 1987, the SACBC had not yet lent their support to sanctions, it would seem that by throwing their weight behind the 1985 Anti-Apartheid bill, the U.S.C.C. was in fact breaking a "sacrosanct" principle of Vatican diplomacy, especially as it relates to inter-church relations. A possible exception would be if the SACBC had sent a "secret signal" on sanctions to the American church.

However, whatever position the U.S.C.C. may have taken on sanctions, it seemed to contradict some of its staff's recollection of the church's stance on sanctions against Pretoria. Confided one: "The sanctions controversy was an embarrassment to us. The bishops were always asking: "What is the position of the South African bishops on sanctions."[479] This embarrassment was exacerbated by the fact that virtually all mainline Protestant churches as well as many Catholic religious congregations supported sanctions.

But even though the U.S.C.C. was in favor of economic sanctions against the apartheid regime, it seemed not to have been involved ad extra. Neither protests nor demonstrations were organized in support of sanctions. In fact a staff person of the U.S.C.C. who took part in a demonstration and was arrested at the South African embassy "went there only as a private citizen, but with the knowledge of his superiors."[480]

But, for another Catholic church group, Network, there was no ambiguity about its position on sanctions against South Africa. Perhaps, among the various Catholic groups, Network is the most progressive and the most consistent in its opposition to Pretoria and to U.S. policy toward the white minority regime. Since its values "include respect for the human dignity of individuals and their rights and the right of self-determination of individuals and nations, Network opposes the apartheid system of the South African government as a violation of these rights."[481] Together with both church-based and secular anti-apartheid groups, it had lent its support to several "Congressional initiatives toward comprehensive sanctions against South Africa in order to move that repressive government toward the dismantling of its inhuman apartheid system." One of those initiatives was S635, the Anti-Apartheid Act of 1985, which would eventually become the Comprehensive Anti-Apartheid Act of 1986.[482]

From the very beginning, Network worked assiduously for the passage of comprehensive sanctions against South Africa. This is understandable since the organization put a higher premium on the struggle against apartheid than on any other African issue. To a large extent, the tactics used were not different from those used during the attempt to repeal the Clark Amendment. The level of intensity was, no doubt, higher.

According to Network, the sanctions bill did not gather momentum "until Dellums picked it up."[483] As stated earlier, opponents of the bill considered it so radical and "unpassable" that they allowed it to be voted on by the House. But, surprisingly, it passed the House overwhelmingly and "set a new threshold for sanctions legislation against Pretoria." Network worked closely with Dellums and his staff on the Comprehensive Anti-Apartheid Act. They held several strategy meetings with the Congressman and his staff. In the Senate, important contacts were Senators Nancy Kasebaum (R-KS), and Pete Dominici (D-New Mexico). In one meeting with Senator Kasebaum, she told a Network lobbyist: "I appreciate what Network does, but I can't vote with you on this one."[484] She did vote for sanctions, however.

Like the U.S.C.C., Network does not take part in protests and demonstrations because as a registered lobby, "it does not make them look good." But unlike the U.S.C.C., neither does it testify at hearings because it is not one of our strongest points." Neither tactic was used on South African sanctions. Most of the face-to-face meetings with Congressmen and Senators would last for about twenty to thirty minutes. Strategy cessions with Congressional staff usually lasted longer.

Coalitional lobbying was a particularly important aspect of Network's lobbying strategy. In this regard, while the church group cooperated with several religious and secular anti-apartheid groups, the role of the Interfaith Center for Corporate Responsibility (ICCR) was crucial in the South African sanctions campaign. The Center is a "mine of information" on the South African economy and the role of U.S. multinational corporations play in oiling the wheels of its apartheid-driven industries.

From January 1985 to October 1986, Network's campaign for the enactment of the Comprehensive Anti-Apartheid Act of 1986 led it to make "twenty-five Senate visits, eighteen House visits, five phone lobbies of the Senate, one phone lobby of the House, two sign-ons, and to send two targeted memos to the Senate, one memo to the full Senate, five mailings to the field and two full phone alerts."[485] One of the targeted memos was sent to the United States Senate Foreign Relations Committee in June 1985. It reminded the members of the Committee that:

> You have the unique opportunity, to shape U.S. foreign policy in such a way that it is consonant with the beliefs and values which underlie our democratic form of government. In the very near future, you will be discussing and marking up the Anti-Apartheid Act of 1985, S635. This legislation imposes moderate economic restrictions on the Republic of South Africa. It significantly alters the administration's policy of 'constructive engagement' which has had little effect in moving the South African government to substantive reform of its apartheid system.[486]

"Network," it continues, "urges you to support S635 and to vote against any measures which delay immediate action."[487]

PROTESTANTS

By their statements as well as activities, the world-wide Anglican communion and its American sister church, the Episcopal Church, have shown themselves to be avowed opponents of white minority rule in South Africa.

As far back as 1970, the Most Rev. Michael Ramsey, Archbishop of Canterbury and the primus inter pares within worldwide Anglicanism, visited South Africa. In a sermon before a multi-racial congregation in St. Mary's Cathedral, Johannesburg, he called apartheid a "hindrance to the church's task of preaching the gospel."[488] He also prodded the Anglican fellowship to include all people "white people, black people, colored people, conservative people, radical people, people with old ideas, and people with new ideas."[489] But in spite of his statements, Ramsey opposed WCC's Fund to Combat Racism reportedly because some of the recipients of the Fund's largesse were engaged in guerrilla activities. The Synod of the Anglican Church of the Province of South Africa also opposed the WCC program. It withheld its annual grant "until the reasons for the financial aid were explained."[490]

But the Episcopal Churchmen for South Africa, headquartered in New York City, called the action an "extraordinary step toward breaking out of the encrusted and unrealistic rigidity which plagues christendom in the West."[491] The Most Rev. Francis Oliver Green-

Wilkinson, Bishop of Zambia and Archbishop of Central Africa, denounced the rulers of South Africa as guilty of a "great lie" when they claim to uphold christian principles. He warned that the greatest danger to christianity in the twentieth century was that it "should be identified with minority rule in the Southern part of Africa."[492]

In the U.S., the Episcopal Church lent its support to the campaign for comprehensive economic sanctions against Pretoria. At its General Convention in Anaheim, California in September 1985, the church "in obedience to our call fearlessly to contend against evil and to make no peace with oppression" voted to "mandate that the Executive Council divest all holdings in companies operating in South Africa" and urged the Church Pension Fund as well as all dioceses, parishes, and other church institutions to "examine its portfolio with a view to identifying and divesting any such holdings."[493] The motion for the adoption of the diocesan version of the resolution was proposed by Rev. Nathaniel Porter, the former Howard University Episcopal Chaplain.[494]

During the debate on comprehensive sanctions at the General Convention, Canon Kwasi Thornell of the Washington Cathedral made a personal call to Tutu in South Africa to ask for his opinion on sanctions.[495] He gave his blessing. Thornell's ploy was meant to "encourage" the General Convention to support sanctions. The Union of Black Episcopalians, a group based in Cincinnati, Ohio, needed no such prodding. In fact, they were the very people who had been assiduously pushing the Episcopal Church to support comprehensive sanctions. The efforts of these anti-apartheid activists helped the church to approve of sanctions, a decision that, undoubtedly, had a positive impact on the overall campaign to pass the 1986 Comprehensive Anti-Apartheid Act.

As stated earlier, the Episcopal Church did not have a Washington, D.C. office until 1979 and did not start lobbying Congress until 1988. "The Episcopal Church did not think it necessary to have a Washington office because it is already powerful and has access to people in government."[496] While other "churches are trying to 'get in,' the Episcopal Church is already in. You may just pick up the phone and call somebody in power."[497]

But when the Episcopal Church lobbies Congress, it begins by first of all developing a relationship with a particular Congressman and then "speaks truth to power." Abrasiveness and caustic language are deemed counterproductive. There is a need to develop a long term "symbiotic relationship" between the church lobbyist and the

Congressman. In speaking the "truth," however, 'humor is the best medicine.' It is imperative to "communicate truth with humor." To be a successful lobbyist, one must have access to the Congressman and his staff. Information paves the road to access. If these rules are followed, it has been found that "when a member of Congress has given his word on something, he has always delivered."[498]

A staff of the Washington office explained the power of humor: There was a bill before Congress which would have deprived the Givichians of Alaska of their hunting rights and their livelihood. Since the Givichians were predominantly Episcopalian, the Episcopal Church took up their case. A key Episcopalian Senator was asked to support the bill in a language laced with humor:

Henry the VIII had a dream nation: that all would be Episcopalian. His dream was fulfilled among the Givichian of Alaska. If you pass this bill, you have destroyed Henry's dream. We couldn't afford to lose a whole nation. And there are not many Episcopalians.[499]

The bill failed. Perhaps, humor had something to do with it. There is no doubt that the Episcopal Church played an important role in the comprehensive sanctions campaign against South Africa. It was a role whose linchpin was the "Tutu-Walker connection."

The Washington, D.C. Diocese of the Episcopal Church took the mandate of the General Conference on South African sanctions very seriously. The main catalyst for this stance was its own head, the late Bishop John Walker, a native of Barnsville, Georgia. This former teacher at the Episcopal Church-owned St. Paul's (Prep) School in Concord, New Hampshire, was well-suited for a style of lobbying different from that of most mainline church anti-apartheid groups. He "was good at bringing people together off-the-record to talk on issues," especially problems of justice and peace. He met such disparate and ideologically-incompatible personalities as Tambo, Buthelezi and the South African ambassador in the U.S. to discuss ways and means of dismantling the apartheid system. At the same time, he was one of the most active bishops of the Episcopal Church.

However, it was not Walker alone but his relationship with Tutu - the "Tutu - Walker connection" - that had an enormous impact on both the comprehensive sanctions campaign and U.S. policy toward South Africa. The relationship between the two men started as a "beneficent accident." Both had met at an orientation seminar for new bishops in

Nairobi, Kenya, in the 1970's, one of many such seminars Walker used to attend.   Consequently, Tutu invited Walker to his Episcopal ordination in South Africa.

Three important bonds cemented the two men's friendship. First, they were politically anti-apartheid activists. Walker was active in TransAfrica, the ACOA, and allied organizations. Tutu was affiliated with the UDF and other South African anti-apartheid organizations. Second, as black men, they had personal experiences of institutional white racism perpetuated as apartheid and Jim Crow. Third, they were two black men who rose professionally in a "predominantly white church -"[500] with all that entails. Both men were also influential - one within the Episcopal/Protestant church and Jewish synagogues, in the U.S., the other worldwide.

Consequently, as the South African sanctions campaign gathered steam in the 1980's, so did the impact of the Tutu-Walker connection. Within South Africa, Tutu, respledescent in his newly-won Nobel Peace Prize, became obviously the premier anti-apartheid leader. Even though he did not sign the Kairos Document, a theological document that has been compared to the "Barmen Declaration in which the confessing church challenged rising Nazism in Germany in 1934,[501] he had, no doubt, impeccable anti-apartheid credentials. On his refusal to sign the now famous document, Tutu told Washington Post correspondent Allister Sparks: "I am in agreement with the broad outline. I am with them maybe 90% of the way."[502] However, he found the tone "unnecessarily abrasive...language."[503] Although he delayed before embracing comprehensive sanctions against Pretoria, his position on foreign investment was unambiguous. In September 1979, he condemned foreign investment for being "supportive of an oppressive system...We do not in fact lack for an improvement in the South African situation. We want fundamental change...[The Sullivan Principles] are ameliorative, they make improvements. They shift the furniture around the room, instead of changing the furniture."[504]

On February 3, 1985, at his enthronement as the first black Anglican Bishop of Johannesburg, the 1984 Nobel Peace Prize Laureate warned: "I give notice that if [within 18 months to two years] apartheid is not being actively dismantled, then...I will myself call for punitive economic sanctions [against South Africa] whatever the legal consequences may be for doing so."[505] However, on April 2, 1986, Tutu called for comprehensive economic sanctions against South Africa:

Our land is burning and bleeding, and so I call on the international community to apply punitive sanctions against the government...I have no hope of real change from this government unless they are forced...We face a catastrophe in this land and only the action of the international community by applying pressure can save us.[506]

In the U.S., Walker was equally active. In 1985, he led some members of his diocese - priests, students, and other lay people - in protest to the South African Embassy, where he was arrested and booked. He also testified at a congressional hearing in 1986 in support of sanctions. Earlier, Walker, Tutu, and Fr. Nathaniel Porter, then the Episcopal Church's chaplain at Howard University, met Chester Crocker, Reagan's Assistant Secretary of State for South Africa, and the "father" of constructive engagement to impress upon him the desire of blacks in the U.S. and in South Africa for comprehensive sanctions against the apartheid regime in Pretoria.[507] The trio received a very cold reception from the former Georgetown Political Science professor, who patronizingly stuck to the well-worn argument that economic sanctions "would hurt blacks." The Tutu-Walker relationship is a good example of christian Pan Africanism as an agent of southern African decolonization. Perhaps, not since Bishop Turner of the AMEC established links with Africa in the 19th century has the relationship between two black men had such an impact on the politics of the U.S. and South Africa.

Of the various churches, the U.C.C. was one of the earliest proponents of the use of the power of "church's purse" to influence U.S. foreign policy. For over three decades, it had shown a growing concern about the role of multi-national corporations in "developing countries,"[508] and about how the funds it invested in them were being used. The Tenth General Synod, building on foundations carefully constructed since 1969 by three successive General Synods,
adopted two concrete recommendations concerning social responsibility in the management of invested funds. The four national instrumentalities that hold the main United Church of Christ-related investment portfolios have found in these recommendations useful guidelines for their special concern with corporations that have large overseas operations.[509]

Of special interest to the Church was the role of U.S. multinationals in southern Africa in general and South Africa in particular. In its Pronouncement on the "The Role of Transnational Business in Mass Economic Development," the Tenth General Synod, while appealing to

American companies to promote fair employment practices, however, "recognizes that such responses by certain U.S. transnational businesses do not really challenge the apartheid system and some are even welcomed by the South African government."[510]

But in spite of its strong opposition to apartheid, the U.C.C. was not one of the first churches to demand total "withdrawal" by U.S. corporations from South Africa until majority-rule was established. In this regard, other church groups were more aggressive than the U.C.C.

> Ford has received such a resolution from the United Presbyterians, General Electric from the Reformed Church in America, and the Women's and the World Divisions of the United Methodist Board for Global Ministries, General Motors for the American Baptists, the Disciples, the Jesuits (Maryland), and the Reformed Church in America, Standard Oil of California from the Disciples and the United Methodist Board for Global Ministries World Division, Texaco from the Disciples, the Reformed Church in America, the Sisters of Charity (N.Y.), and the United Methodist Board for Global Ministries World Division.[511]

While the U.C.C. held stock in all five multinationals, when "asked to co-sponsor one or more of these resolutions and to vote their proxies for them all",[512] the church hesitated. The Eleventh General Synod recommended "increased attention by members and organizations of the United Church of Christ during the biennium 1977-1979 to the critical ethical questions raised by many recent disclosures concerning business practices in the United States society."[513] The U.C.C. also called on the N.C.C. to bring together representatives of business and church leaders in a continuing dialogue

> to examine the moral bases of current corporate business practice...to evaluate the ability and willingness of the corporations to serve the domestic and international social goals of our nation...to appraise the positive and negative effects of transnational business on the development of a new and fairer international economic order.[514]

The role of U.S. companies in South Africa was of special concern to the Church. It was a concern it acted upon when the Fifteenth General Synod called on the U.C.C. to "...begin immediately the process of divestment, and to complete divestment within two years."[515]

Given her special interest in the "economic base of oppression," it is not surprising that the struggle to pass the Comprehensive Anti-Apartheid Act (CAAA) of 1986 propelled the U.C.C. into greater activism than ever before on an African issue. Right from the beginning of the Reagan administration, the U.C.C., like most other church groups, had viewed with concern and alarm the tilt of U.S. policy toward Pretoria as symbolized by constructive engagement.

However, it was not until the Free South Africa Movement turned into a juggernaut that the Church gave a more concerted and increased attention to the drive to impose comprehensive economic sanctions against the apartheid regime in South Africa. From April to September, 1986, it was the major issue that involved the total commitment of the U.C.C.[516] The Church was involved in all the late "pre-vote maneuver of U.S. anti-apartheid groups prior to the enactment of the CAAA. For example, it took part in the "lobby day" organized by the WOA, in which about two-hundred local anti-apartheid activists from across the nation came to Washington, D.C. to pressure Congress to pass the CAAA. Having arrived two days before the vote in the House, they went from door to door and personally asked the Congressmen and their staff to support the imposition of comprehensive economic sanctions against South Africa. Among these were some pastors, who lobbied Congress virtually everyday until the enactment of the CAAA. The personal experiences of partner churches, who were still suffering from the violence of the apartheid state, were used to impress on Congressmen the need and urgency of passing sanctions that would "bite." U.C.C. staff also did five "fact sheets" on comprehensive economic sanctions against Pretoria and sent them to several Congressmen.[517]   Like Network, it was the introduction of Dellums' bill, which more than any other factor, galvanized the U.C.C. into increased action. For not only did the Church view it as a progressive piece of legislation, it was also seen as potentially "passable." The Dellums' bill passed the House by voice vote in a move now recognized as a "political faux pas" by its opponents and a blessing by its proponents.

The U.C.C. also worked on CAAA in the Senate before it was debated and passed by that body. A clever tactic adopted by the Church was the use of "instant information," a clear indication that we truly now live in a "global village." As the fate of the CAAA hung in the balance in the Senate, U.C.C. staff "phoned a partner church" in South Africa for information on developments within the country. The information gathered was typed and faxed to Congress. An incident that must have had an impact on Congressmen and Senators was when one of the churches reported that it had been invaded by South African troops because it was "communist."[518] In their lobbying efforts to pass the CAAA, the U.C.C. was also joined by some of its staff from its New York office.

CONCLUDING COMMENT

The passage of the CAAA was a milestone in the struggle by the African majority for the full restoration of a freedom that was violently taken away from them after the first Europeans settled in their land over three centuries earlier. The installation of Mandela as the first black president of South Africa, which was a culmination of this struggle, was celebrated all over the country. In Soweto, a symbol of apartheid violence as well as a cradle of African resistance and resilence, the residents "took to the streets in jubilant dance, singing songs of an epic struggle for liberation."[15] And dignitories from more than 150 countries came to applaud the end of apartheid and to honor "one of the world's rare heroes and one of history's sweetest victories over racial subjugation."[16]

CHAPTER VI - SUMMARY

This study of U.S. southern Africa policy was organized around three specific anti-colonial bills passed by the U.S. Congress within a fifteen year period and the roles played by American churches in the noble process of lobbying for enactment of progressive legislation. The questions and problems posed by the study have been raised in the introductory chapter. One of those questions is basic: As the spiritual and moral leaders of the country, have American church groups used their potentially immense religious, human, and material resources to pressure U.S. policy makers to adopt a more "christian," humane, and progressive policy in southern Africa? Or, were they, as their critics claim, "advance troops of colonialism and imperialism? Thus, this concluding chapter will seek to answer the questions raised through a synthesis of the key case study findings, especially when they can be generalized. An attempt will also be made to point out the implications of the findings to the traditional views of U.S. southern Africa policy as well as to the theories of group interest on foreign policy making. The hope is that suggestions for future research on church group influence on U.S. southern Africa policy will be undertaken.

U.S. SOUTHERN AFRICA POLICY AND AMERICAN CHURCH GROUP INTERESTS AND FOREIGN POLICY PREFERENCES

As stated in Chapter I, the first hypothesis claims that U.S. South Africa policy significantly reflects the interests and foreign policy preferences of American Catholic and Protestant groups. To most church critics, these two church groups have the same interests and foreign policy preferences as the U.S. government. Moreover, in spite of the constitutional requirements of the separation of church and state, they argue that American churches have traditionally enjoyed an exceedingly stable and collaborative relationship with the government, especially in the foreign policy arena. For example, until Vietnam, most of these churches have wholeheartedly lent their support to virtually all of America's wars. This cozy relationship was aptly described by a high-ranking Catholic clergyman asked to comment on the massive American military build-up in the early years of the Vietnam war, the late Cardinal Francis Spellman of New York replied: "My country, may it always be right. Right or wrong, my country."[519] In the 1930's Dorothy Day, the founder of the radical Catholic Worker movement, had called on the church to "end its connivance with the oppression of the poor, the worker, the Negro, the Mexican, and the Filipino by our industrial capitalist order."[520]   However, while the American Catholic Church and other mainline churches have in more recent times enunciated policies contrary to those of U.S. policy, the old image of the churches as agents of the U.S. government has remained intact in the eyes of some of its critics.

However, it is obvious that American church groups do have interests and policy preferences on southern African issues. But, they, in no way, reflect those of the United States. At least, the official statements of American church groups on southern Africa testify to that fact. In the Rhodesia/Zimbabwe case, for example, with the exception of the period when the U.S. was in compliance with U.N. sanctions against the white minority regime, American church group interests and policy preferences have consistently been at variance with those of the U.S. government. Among the churches themselves, obvious similarities exist between their policy preferences as well as their interests. This may be as a result of the strong biblical principles, which inform official church statements, especially on issues of justice and peace. Even then, there was a difference in the tenor of some church pronouncements: a church like the U.C.C. was often more "hard-hitting" than the others in its "prophetic witness" in southern Africa.

An analysis of the case studies also revealed that American church groups were interested in each of the southern African cases. But the degree of interest differed from one issue to the other. For example, while the WOA, the USCC, and UMC were active on Rhodesian sanctions, Network was not. On its own part, WOA not only issued statements in support of Rhodesian sanctions, it went further. It acted as both the coordinator and "catalyzing agent" in the struggle to repeal the Byrd Amendment. The interest of the UMC also went beyond the spiritual-moral and humanitarian concerns. It has important partner churches with thousands of members and many institutions in Rhodesia. Two of its members, Muzorewa and Banana, were to influence not only their fellow Methodists in the U.S. and Rhodesia but to have some impact on U.S. policy.

The interest of the Catholic Church was similar to that of the UMC. As early as the 1940's, the CAIP had ably articulated the moral and humanitarian concerns of Catholics, concerns that the U.S.C.C. has reinforced over the years. The Church also had a larger membership and more institutions than, perhaps, any other denomination in the country. Most importantly, it had Bishop Lamont, a prophetic clergyman, who had credibility in Rhodesia, in America, and all over the world. Most importantly, there was a symbiotic relationship between the Rhodesian Catholic Conference and the National Conference of Catholic Bishops as well as the Rhodesian Peace and Justice Committee and the U.S.C.C. This relationship is a key to an understanding of the Church's support for the repeal of the Byrd Amendment. Unfortunately, even though the NCCB had been given the "go-ahead" to lobby for sanctions by the Rhodesian bishops, there was no serious attempt either on the part of the NCCB or the USCC to mobilize the laity in support of sanctions against the white minority regime in Salisbury (Harare). There seems to have been a lack of awareness that "we are tied to a political system by our habits of consumption, by our compliance with laws, by our avoidance of conflict, by our membership in certain classes and groups. In varying degrees,...we are all implicated in the follies and crimes of those who govern us."[521] Most American Catholics, however, seem to have seen things differently.

GROUP INFLUENCE THROUGH SOCIAL AND INTELLECTIVE PROCESSES

The second hypothesis of this study states that groups are more likely to influence decisions made by social processes than those made by intellective processes. In each of the three cases studied, social as well as intellective processes were at play. However, the predominant style was social. And that was responsible for the level of access that church groups had to policy makers. As stated earlier, with the exception of the Carter administration, regular church group access to the executive branch was highly limited or non-existent during the four presidencies that encompass this study. And even during the Carter White House, church group access to policy makers as well as a coincidence of interests between the two was not always a foregone conclusion. For example, as soon as Brzezinski's anticommunism began to supersede Young's pro-black Africanism in the middle of the Carter administration, the churches soon found some of their policies in conflict with those of the White House. A good example of this conflict was the attempt by Carter to repeal the Clark Amendment and resume covert military aid to UNITA. In the executive branch where decisions are usually made by the intellective process, it is extremely difficult for groups to have any influence in such an environment.

Consequently, the only alternative left for church groups was Congress, the ultimate environment where decisions are made by social processes. "In making their legislative decisions, members of Congress are influenced by numerous pressures - from their constituents, the White House, the news media, lobbyists and organized interest groups, and their own party leadership and colleagues on Capitol Hill. These pressures are a central feature of the congressional environment...All these pressures are present in varying degrees in every step of the legislative process; the interests and influence of groups and individuals outside Congress have a considerable impact on the fate of a bill on Capitol Hill."[522]

It is also interesting to note how the internal structure of the various churches affected their input in the foreign policy decision-making process. For example, churches like the U.C.C. and UMC (the UMC has a middle class background), which are highly decentralized and democratic in their institutional structure, tended to be more aggressive in utilizing the advantages afforded interest groups by the congressional process than the more centralized Catholic and Episcopal churches. Even then, differences exist between the latter as to the modalities of democratic participation in foreign policy decision-making. Studies have shown that in spite of its highly centralized nature, the Catholic Church is not monolithic.[523]

One of the findings of this study is that it also applies to the realm of foreign policy. The divergent policy positions taken by the U.S.C.C. on the one hand, and Network and some religious congregations on the other, testify to that fact. Generally, Network and Catholic religious organizations are likely to be more liberal, progressive, and activist on foreign policy than the U.S.C.C. Among Episcopalians, local dioceses are expected to carry out the foreign policy mandates of the General Convention. However, the speed with which they are carried out is left to the discretion of local dioceses. On southern Africa, for example, the diocese of Washington under the late Bishop Walker set the tone for the whole church. In this sense, groups are not unlike individuals. Just as a person's character affects his interaction with the outside world, so it is with the churches. As corporate personalities, their internal characteristics influence their external behavior. Thus, if the churches hope to gain more access to inject their moral/ethical and humanitarian norms into the decision-making process, do they have to reform themselves and become more democratic?

This, obviously, poses two problems for the church as well as for the larger society. The first problem is the relationship between the Washington, D.C.-based church activists and the national congregations. In his book The Growing Church Lobby in Washington, James Adams has observed that most mainline church activists are out of touch with their fellow congregants. They also tend to be more liberal on issues than their predominantly conservative fellow church members.[524] By his statement, Adams seems to infer that if the churches are to be faithful to their democratic roots, the opinions and positions of church activists ought to mirror those of their conservative constituency. What Adams has failed to understand is that while a more democratized church in which church activists are sensitive to the opinions of their membership may be welcome, it should be realized that, as an ideology, christianity is based on certain moral and ethical principles which are not amenable to majority veto.

One of those principles legitimized church interest and activism in the three cases studied in this research: the right of a people to reclaim their national territory taken from them by force even if it meant the application of adequate force to achieve this objective. Thus, while this writer has great admiration for the Gandhis and the Martin Luther Kings, he firmly believes that but for the application of "adequate force" by African guerrillas in southern Africa, Mozambique, Guinea-Bissau, Angola, Zimbabwe, Namibia would not be free today. The same is also true of South Africa. In fact, but for the threat of black violence in South Africa, it is most unlikely that the white minority would have voted so overwhelmingly to enter into negotiations with the black majority for the transfer of power. In the U.S., even though the late Martin Luther King, Jr. has been raised to the level of a national icon, it is becoming increasingly obvious to many African Americans that but for the emergence of Malcolm X, replete with the threat of using "any means necessary" - including "bullet power" - to achieve equal rights, it is doubtful that the white power structure would have relented and made changes. King would still have been called "uppity" and a "trouble-maker." Black South Africans, therefore, should not kid themselves. As Frederick Douglas put it: "Power concedes nothing without demand. It never has. It never will."

The second problem is constitutional and canonical. Constitutionally, there is fear that political activism by the churches would breach the wall of separation between the church and the state, which would breed social disorder.

> The history of religious persecution (and its contemporary horror) teach that justice and human dignity require that religious belief be protected from public coercion and that public space be protected from the violence engendered by religious passion.[525]

In a bid to restrain the churches, the Internal Revenue Service (IRS) had issued a "rule which held that tax exempt organizations (See 501{C}{3}) such as the United Church of Christ...could not publish voting records. To do so would jeopardize their tax exempt status on the grounds that the tax status prohibited such organizations from direct participation in electoral politics."[526] The U.C.C. sued and within weeks, the IRS issued a letter stating that "publishing the voting record as stipulated did not jeopardize the tax-exempt status of the U.C.C."[527] However, others like Chief Justice William Rehnquist have declared that "the wall of separation between church and state is a metaphor based on bad history. It should be frankly and explicitly abandoned."[528] This writer opines that the separation of church and state should not hinder cooperation between the two bodies, especially in the promotion of progressive policies.

The canonical problem arises out of the ambiguity inherent in some of the norms and directives guiding the roles of priest-activists, especially Catholic priests, within the political process. It is an ambiguity that is evident in the requirements of Canon 287, paragraph 2 of the Code of Canon Law, the universal law of the Catholic Church, which states that "clerics are not to have an active role in political parties and in the direction of labor unions unless the need to protect the rights of the Church or to promote the common good requires it in the judgement of the competent ecclesiastical authority."[529] This law has been the bane of Catholic priests-politicians around the world. In the U.S., it led to the forced retirement from Congress of Fr. Robert Drinan, the former Jesuit Congressman from Massachusetts. In Nicaragua, it led to a clash between the "radical" Sandinista priests, like former Foreign Minister Miguel d' Escoto and his compatriots, and the Vatican. In Nigeria, the ecclesiastical authorities have "gone after" Fr. Moses Adasu, the country's first Catholic priest-governor (Benue State),[530] who had been elected not only because the people believed he would not "eat their money" but because they saw him as someone who could defend them against the threat of a resurgent Muslim fundamentalism.[531] In Haiti, Fr. Betrande Aristide, the exiled president of the Caribbean nation, also fell afoul of the Catholic Church hierarchy as a result of his political activities. In fact, had Aristide received the full and active support of the ecclesiastical authorities, as Aquino did in the Philippines, he would still be president of Haiti today and the nascent Haitian democracy would have survived. High Catholic ecclesiastical authorities have dissuaded the U.S. Catholic hierarchy from helping president Aristide.[532] It is the opinion of this writer that the church's directive on priest and politics has one thing in common with her policy on the foreign policy behavior of various national churches: it is regressive and helps to perpetuate the status quo.

Really, it is very similar to the attitude of the U.S. toward the "developing countries." While these church directives might suit "developed countries," where the bureaucracies are much more stable and controlled, and the legal systems more mature and impersonal, they may not apply in the so-called "Third World," where personal rule, even in democracies, is still common,[533] and progressive change is often possible only through the charismatic leader. Archbishop Denis Hurley, the former Ordinary of Durban diocese and the ex-president of the southern African Bishop's Conference, was so confused about the ban on political activism among the clergy that he asked Pope John Paul II for clarification.[534] Interviewed by National Catholic News Service on January 27, 1987 during the episcopal conference's meeting in Pretoria, South Africa, he confirmed that he had asked the Pope some years ago to issue a substantial document on the issue. He said he wanted a papal explanation of the difference between pursuing political power and promoting morality in political life. Hurley said that the papal ban is ambiguous and could be used by the white South African government and conservative Catholics in his country to accuse the bishops of being "out of tune with the Vatican" and pressure them to "stop criticizing the government."[535] The Pope did not reply to his letter.[536]

GROUP RESOURCES AND THE MAKING OF FOREIGN POLICY

The third hypothesis states that the ability of groups to influence foreign policy depends on their resources and other factors. As stated earlier, the measurement of influence has always been problematic. But all the same, influence-peddling gurus in the nation's capital can testify to some of the characteristics of Washington, D.C.'s powerful interest groups and the men and women who run them. Many of them have their headquarters on K Street in Washington, D.C., which the New York Times calls "the equivalent of a new branch of government."[537] Some of the prime offices on this famous street cost up to $22,000 per month.[538] Powerful interest groups like the American Israel Public Affairs Committee (AIPAC) and the National Rifle Association (NRA) often have multi-million dollar budgets and hundreds of staff.[539] They have easy access to Congressmen not only as a result of the generous contributions these groups make to their campaigns, but also because they often pose an electoral threat.

But the church groups studied are different from the powerful and popular secular interest groups in many ways. In fact, one of the most interesting results from the three cases studied is the disparity between the material resources available to church interest groups and the level of access they have to Congressmen and their staff. Of the five church groups involved in this study, only the U.S.C.C., now ensconced in its new and opulent headquarters near the Catholic University of America, can boast of truly comfortable staff offices. Compared to the powerful secular interest groups, church groups are understaffed and under financed. Given these obvious disabilities, why do they still have such easy access to Congressmen? "Access is the first arrow in any lobbyist's quiver, especially lobbyists of the old breed. Scores of times I have been told that votes are won simply by gaining an audience with a time-harassed congressman, so he could hear your case."[540] Why were they able to help in changing U.S. policy in Rhodesia and South Africa and not in Angola?

A Network staff explained her organization's efforts in this fashion: "We look like them, act like them, but have a different message. Congress has respect for Network because they know you are not there to grease their palms, that you are prepared and that you are coming from a moral and ethical perspective."[541]   An Episcopalian lobbyist sees the church's potential influence in the silent power of moral force as symbolized by Christ's resurrection after his victory over death. According to him, it was this moral force that transformed Vaclav Havel from prisoner to the president of Czechoslovakia, Arpard Gontz from prison to the Hungarian president, and Boris Yeltsin from a political pariah to the highest office in Russia.[542]   For too long, he lamented, U.S. foreign policy has been guided by the concept of the "massa damna" (the damned masses) and the elect as espoused by Augustine and Niebuhr.   According to this warped theosophy, Americans are the elect of God while her enemies are already condemned by the Almighty. So, in a war between the U.S. and her enemies, moral or ethical norms do not apply since God has already "damned them." He cited as an example the barbarity of the apartheid system in South Africa and the massacre of Iraqi troops during Operation Desert Storm. He stated that the churches have the power and obligation to infuse moral principles in the formulation and implementation of U.S. foreign policy.

Consequently,the ability of church groups to influence U.S. foreign policy depends, to a large extent, on their willingness to use moral suasion. In some cases, economic and rational arguments were used. The presence of a credible and charismatic clergyman from the affected country lends credibility to the moral argument and the influence of American church groups on foreign policy. According to a former staff of WOA, U.S. churches "are more likely to get involved in an issue if an important clergyman from a partner church visits them and asks for help. Churches respond more to people than to causes." During the Rhodesian crisis, for example, the activities of Lamont and Muzorewa[543] in the U.S. and in their own country had a significant impact on U.S. Catholic and Methodist churches in their opposition to the Byrd Amendment. In the struggle against apartheid, there is no gainsaying the fact that Tutu's visits to the U.S. encouraged both the Episcopal Church and the American people to support comprehensive economic sanctions against South Africa. In Angola from where no prominent clergyman emerged to communicate with U.S. churches, the Clark Amendment was repealed.   Could there be a connection? Perhaps, the most important finding from this study is that neither money nor staff nor cozy offices alone make an interest group powerful. Thus, given their relatively lean resources and the level of access church groups have to U.S. policy makers on southern Africa issues when compared with the better staffed and funded secular interest groups, it may be said that not so often have interest groups done so much with so little to influence South Africa policy.

Finally, the study of the three cases reveals a not so surprising reality. If, for Tip O'Neil, 'all politics is local,' it may be said that for the church "most politics is institutional," even in the foreign policy arena. Of the five .church groups involved in the study, the two wealthiest, Catholics and Episcopalians, displayed an unusual symmetry in their overall attitude toward southern Africa issues, especially on the Comprehensive Anti-Apartheid Act of 1986. While both often used very strong language to condemn the apartheid system, they were less likely to mobilize their members against a policy they oppose. Both rarely engaged in protests or demonstrations. They were, however, more likely to contact higher officials either in the executive or legislative branches or both. This attitude, according to Baum, is due to the "logic of maintenance" as opposed to the "logic of mission," two "logics" operative in every organization. The "logic of mission" nudges the church to be faithful to its raison d'etre, aim and purpose. An important mission of the church is the "preferential option for the poor." The logic of maintenance demands that the

> church protect its international unity...protect its internal cohesion... protect the authority of the ecclesiastical government...protect its economic base, and this often prompts popes and bishops to manifest their solidarity with the powerful and affluent sectors of society, again putting them at odds with the preferential option for the poor.[544]

One of the purposes of this investigation is to fill a research lacuna in the available literature on American interest groups and U.S. foreign policy. While scholars have traditionally analyzed the role and influence of both governmental and non-governmental interest groups on U.S. Foreign Policy, very little attempt has been made to study systematically and comparatively the influence of American religious groups in the shaping and implementation of U.S. foreign policy. Available studies of the impact of American religious groups on U.S. policy have often been hobbled by bias, contradictions, excessive caution, unsubstantiated generalizations, and abysmal ignorance of the role religious groups can, and should, play in forging a more just and humane American foreign policy.

Both Dahl and Almond exemplify the confusion among scholars as to the "proper" place and role of religious groups in the shaping of U.S.

foreign policy. While one identifies a religious group as exercising foreign policy influence "out of all proportion to its size," the other sees religious leaders as incompetent actors in the American Foreign policy process. This study attempted to discover the empirical truth.

Among scholars, the role of religious groups as agents of political stability and change is equally controversial. Critics of religious groups see the challenge of political change as their "Achilles heel," especially since they have historically been known to support the status quo. In fact, one of the reasons why this writer embarked on this study is to find out the role of American churches, especially the Catholic Church, on southern African issues. For, on several occasions, on discovering his profession, even mere strangers have rudely told him: "Your church supports apartheid!" Fortunately, this study has shown that in spite of their disabilities, American churches have made some contributions to African decolonization - at least in recent decades. However, not until they realize and utilize the potential power of moral and ethical norms in American politics will they be able to radically transform the formulation and implementation of U.S. foreign policy.

All the same, other than the problem of influence, which was discussed earlier, this study posed other challenges. First, even though this writer may be considered a "church insider," it was not always easy to have access to relevant information. Second, with perhaps the possible exception of Network, most church groups kept no systematic up-to-date records on their lobbying activities. And, it was not always easy for most of the staff interviewed to recall some important details. While it is true that activity per se is not tantamount to influence, it is equally correct to state that in politics also, "actions speak louder than words." This writer strongly suggests that scholars, especially those involved in the study of religion and politics, link up with church lobbyists to develop modalities for recording their activities. This will obviously facilitate the study of religion and politics, two phenomena that are intertwined and present in all civilizations. With the crisis of communism and the end of bipolarity, religion will become an increasingly powerful factor in national and international politics. So, as we come to the end of the 20th century and prepare to enter a new millennium, political scientists and other social scientists should heed the words of Gandhi: "If you think religion has nothing to do with politics, you do not know anything about politics."

ENDNOTES

0.   Henry F. Jackson,
      From the Congo to Soweto,
      New York, Quill, 1984, p. 226.

1.   ibid, p. 170.

2.   West Africa,12-18 October 1992, p. 1706

3.   The Washington Post, December 10, 1992, P. A39.

4.   West Africa, op. cit., p. 1734

5.   Clare Pedrick, "Unlikely Negotiator Help Mozambique Find
      Peace", The Washington Post, October 10, 1992, P.A.

6.   Ernie Regehr, Perceptions of Apartheid, The Churches and
      Political Change in South Africa, (Scottsdale, Pennsylvania,
      Herald Press, 1979), p. 132.

7.   ibid., pp. 42-45.

8.   ibid.

9.   ibid.

10.   "South African Destabilization," U.N. Commission for Africa, 1989,
      p. 16.

11.   ibid., p. 6.

12.   "South Africa Destabilization," Africa Recovery, (UN), October 14, 1989, p.
      1.

13.   "South Africa Destabilization," op. cit., p. 3.

14.   Colin Legum, "The International Moral Protest" in Gwendolen M. Carter and
      Patrick O'Meara (eds) International Politics in Southern Africa, (Bloomington,

Indiana University Press), 1982, pp. 227-228.

15. ibid.

16. Ronald Walters, "Beyond Sanctions, A Comprehensive U.S. Policy for Southern Africa," Word Policy Journal, Winter 1986-87, p. 1.

17. Department of State Background Notes, South Africa, July 1973, p. 9.

18. Jackson, op. cit., p. 245.

19. ibid., p. 38.

20. Ross K. Baker, "Toward a New Constituency for a More Active American Foreign Policy for Africa," Issue, Vol. III, No. 1, Spring 1973, p. 12.

21. Roy M. Melbourne, "The American Response to the Nigerian Conflict, 1968," Issue, Vol. III, No. 1, Spring 1972, pp. 40-41.

22. ibid., p. 38.

23. ibid.

24. Robert N. Bellah and Earl H. Brill, "Religious Influence on United States Foreign Policy," in Michael P. Hamilton (ed), American Character and Foreign Policy, (Grand Rapids, Michigan, Williams B. Eardmans Publishing Co., 1986), p. 55. See also Winthrop S. Hudson, Nationalism and Religion in America, New York, Harper and Row, 1970: States that American missionary enterprise was also to impart the "blessings of American civil and religious liberty."

25. ibid., p. 57.

26. Sylvia M. Jacobs (ed), Black Americans and the Missionary Movement in Africa, (Westport, Connecticut), 1982, p. 8.

27. E. Regehr, Perceptions of Apartheid, The Churches and Political Change in South Africa, (Scottsdale, Pennsylvania, Heralds Press), p. 132.

28. Clarence Clendenen, Robert Collins and Peter Durignam, American in Africa, 1865-1900, Stanford, California, Stanford University, 1964, p. 114.

29. Carol A. Page, "Colonial Reaction to AME Missionaries in South Africa, 1889-1910" in Jacobs, op. cit., p. 9.

30. Frederick B. Bridgman, "The Ethiopian Movement in South Africa," The Missionary Review of the World, Vol. 27, June 1984, p. 441.

31. In November 1787, the African members of the Methodist Society of Philadelphia met to discuss the issue of racism in their church and the need to establish their own church. In 1816, the AME Church took organic form.

32. Bridgman, op. cit., p. 434.

33. J. Muter Chirenje, Ethiopianism and Afro-Americans in Southern Africa, 1883-1916, (LSU Press, 1987), p. 55.

34. ibid., p. 62.

35. ibid., p. 63.

36. ibid.

37. ibid.

38. Carol A. Page, "Colonial Reaction to AME Missionaries in South Africa, 1898-1910," in Jacobs, op. cit., p. 9. For privileges given to African-Americans in South Africa, see E. Dewaal, "American Black Residents and Visitors in S.A.R. before 1899," South African Historical Journal, (November 1974), pp. 52-55.

39. Tony Martin, "Some Reflections on Evangelical Pan Africanism," in Page, op. cit., p. 191.

40. Brian Willan, Sol Plaatje, (Los Angeles, University of California Press, no date), p. 15.

41. ibid.

42. ibid.

43. David Hanuck, Two Decades of Debate: The Controversy Over U.S. Companies in South Africa, (Washington, D.C., Investor Responsibility Research Center, 1983), p. 8.

44. Bridgman, op. cit., p. 438.

45. Jackson, op. cit., p. 133. See also Robert I. Rothbert (ed) Rebellion in Africa, (London, Oxford University Press, 1971), pp. 133-163.

46. It is ironical that before desegregation in the U.S., African students also enjoyed certain privileges denied African-Americans.

47. Chirenje, op. cit., p. 76.

48. H.E. McCalhoum to Chamberlain, April 23, 1902, Public Record Office, London, C.O. 179-224 in Page, op. cit., p. 187.

49. ibid., p. 183.

50. James A. Reichley, Religion in American Public Life, (Washington, D.C., The Brooking Institution, 1985), p. 186.

51. New Catholic Encyclopedia, Vol. IV, Maguire Hill Col, 1965, p. 443.

52. Felician A. Foy and Rose M. Avato (eds), 1990 Catholic Almanac, (Huntington, Indiana, Our Sunday Quarterly Inc 1990), p. 176.

53. ibid.

54. George W. Shepherd, Anti-Apartheid, Transactional Conflict and Western Policy in the Liberation of South Africa, (Westport, Connecticut, Greenwood Press, 1977), p. 33.

55. ibid.

56. Bernard M. Magubane, The Ties That Bind, (Trenton, N.J. Africa World Press, 1987), p. 211.

57. ibid.

58. Shepherd, op.cit.

59. It should be noted that while the cooperation of church and state in the colonial enterprise is undeniable, some clergymen opposed colonialism and slavery, and promoted the rights of the indigenous population.

60. Juis B. Serapiao, "The Roman Catholic Church and the Principle of Self-Determination," Journal of Church and State, Vol. 23, No. 2, 1981, p. 325.

61. Afriano Moreira, The Spirit of Prince Henry and Portugals' Present Policy Overseas, (Lisbon, 1960), p. 27.

62. Luis Marques, Overseas Provinces on Colonies, (Lisbon, 1961), p. 9.

63. Luis B. Serapiao, "The Preaching of Portuguese Colonialism and the Protest of the White Fathers," Issue, Vol. II, No. 1, Spring, 1972, p. 34.

64. Serapiao, op. cit., p. 334.

65. Reichley, op. cit., p. 294.

66. In the U.S., the Vatican once intervened privately in the 1970's to "kill" a progressive statement by the Catholic hierarchy on South Africa, and publicly in the 1980's to modify the bishop's pastoral letter on nuclear weapons. Another example of the Vatican's support for the status quo, could be seen by the secret support the papal nuncio in Manila, Philippines gave to President Marcos, while the local church under Cardinal Sin mobilized the people in support of the Philippine's "democratic revolution."

67. Bulletin of the National Catholic Welfare Conference, March 27, 1927, Vol. III, p. 17.

68. Martin J. Bane, et al., Symposium on Africa, New York, CAIP, 1947, p. 7.

69. ibid., p. 16.

70. ibid., p. 17.

71. ibid., p. 16.

72. Shepherd, op. cit., p. 36.

73. "CAIP Statement on Rhodesia," December, 1965, p. 1.

74. ibid.

75. CAIP News, Vol. XXIII, No. 4, March 21, 1967, p. 1.

76. ibid., p. 2.

77. Reichley, op. cit., p. 253.

78. L. Newbegin, The Relevance of the Trinitarian Doctrine for Today's Mission, (London, Edinburgh Press, 1963), p. 12.

79. ibid., p. 252.

80. David Patton, <u>Christian Mission and the Judgement of God</u>, (London, SCM Press, 1953), pp. 438-439.

81. <u>Origins</u>, Augus 29, 1985, Vol. 15, No. 11, p. 171.

82. <u>ibid</u>., p. 163.

83. <u>The Church and Racism: Toward A More Fraternal Society</u>, Origin, February 23, 1989, Vol. 18, No. 37, p. 614.

84. <u>ibid</u>., p. 615.

85. <u>ibid</u>., p. 617.

86. David McKay, <u>The World, The West and Pretoria</u>, (New York, Co., Inc., 1977), p. 160.

87. Shepherd, <u>op. cit</u>., p. 44.

88. <u>ibid</u>.

89. <u>ibid</u>.

90. <u>ibid</u>., p. 122.

91. <u>ibid</u>., p. 44.

92. <u>ibid</u>., p. 44.

93. The Catholic Church has not always looked kindly to the embrace of marxist/communist philosophy by many southern Africa liberation groups. It should, however, be noted that these liberation groups are primarily African nationalist groups, who turned only to the communist bloc after being rebuffed by the West.

94. See C.W. Hall, "Must our churches finance revolutions?" <u>Reader's Digest</u>, October 1971 and "Which way the world council of churches?" <u>Reader's Digest</u>, November 1971.

95. <u>Christian Century</u>, September 21, 1970.

96. Sheik R. Ali. <u>Southern Africa, An American Enigma</u>, (New York, Praeger, 1987), p. 136.

97. <u>Washington Post</u>, June 24, 1990, p. a22.

98. Philip V. White, "The Black American Constituency for   Southern Africa, 1940-1980," in Alfred Hero, Jr. and John Barrat (eds), The American People and Southern Africa, (Indiana, Lexington Press, 1981), p. 94.

99. Albert J. Menendez, "Religious Lobbies," Liberty, Vol. 77, March-April, 1982, p. 3.

100. E.E. Schattschneider, The Semi-Sovereign People, (New York, Holt, Rinehard and Winston, 1960), p. 35.

101. Robert A. Dahl, "On removing certain impediments to democracy in the United States" in Demetrios Caraley and Mary Epstein (eds), The Making of American Foreign and Domestic Policy, (New York, General Health Publishing Corp.   1978), p. 31.

102. Jack L. Walker, "A Critique of the Elitist Theory of Democracy" in Marian D. Irish et al., Readings in the Politics of American Democracy, (Englewood, Cliffs, New Jersey, Prentice-Hall, Inc., 1969), p. 75.

103. M.P. Hamilton, (ed). American Character and Foreign Policy, (Grand Rapids, Michigan, William B. Earlmans Publishing Co.,   1986), p. 66.

104. The Federalist, (New York, The Modern Library), p.54.

105. ibid., p. 56.

106. David B. Truman, The Governmental Process (2nd edition), (New York, Alfred A. Knopf, 1971) p. ix.

107. V. O. Key. Public Opinion and American Democracy, (New York, Alfred A. Knopf, 1961), p. 500.

108. Henry V. Ehrmann, "Interest Groups," 1968 International Encyclopedia of the Social Sciences, vii, pp. 486-487.

109. Franz Neumann, The Democratic and the Authoritarian State, (no city and publisher, 1957), pp. 12-14.

110. Harold J. Laski. The American Democracy, (New York, The Viking Press, 1948), p. 313.

111. Quoted in Truman, op. cit., p. 51.

112. Theodore J. Loevi. The End of Liberalism, (New York, W.W. Norton and

Company, 1979), pp. 58-59.

113. Mansur Olson. The Logic of Collective Action, (Cambridge, Massachusetts, Havard University Press, 1971), p. 2.

114. Michael Parenti. Democracy for the Few, (New York, St. Martin's Press, 1977), p. 316.

115. Philip M. Stern. The Best Congress Money Can Buy, (New York, Random House, Inc., 1988), pp. 36-37.

116. Richard C. Snyder, Richard C., H.W. Bruck, and Burton Sapin, "Decision-Making as an Approach to the Study of International Politics," Foreign Policy Decision-Making: An Approach to the Study of International Politics, ed. by Richard Snyder et al (New York, the Free Press, 1962), pp. 14-185.

117. Harold Karan Jacobson and William Zimmerman, "Approaches to the Analysis of Foreign Policy," The Shaping of Foreign Policy, (New York, Atherton Press, 1969), p. 7. The most comprehensive review of the analyses of foreign policy behavior is Kenneth Waltz' Man, State and War, (New York,   Columbia University Press, 1969). See also J. David Singer and Arnold Wolfers, "the Level of Analysis Problem in International Relations," World Politics, XIV:1, October 1961, pp. 77-92, and "Discord and collaboration: Essays on International Politics," (Baltimore, The Johns Hopkins Press, Maryland, 1962), pp. 3-24.

118. Dahl, Robert A. Congress and Foreign Policy, (New York, Harcourt Brace and Co., 1950), p. 261

119. ibid., p. 56.

120. Almond, Gabriel A., The American People and Foreign Policy, (New York, Frederick A. Praeger Publishers, 1960), p. 50.

121. ibid., pp. 140-141.

122. ibid.

123. Cohen, Bernard C., The Influence of Non-Governmental Groups on Foreign Policy-Making, (Boston, World Peace Foundation, 1959), p. 1.

124. Herbert A. Simon, ("Notes on the Observation and Measurement of Political Power," J. of Politics, Vol. 15, No. 4, November 1953), states that the position of a powerful interest group "may be so well-known

and so important to policy makers that they are constrained to take it into account in their first formulation of policy," and is therefore, almost impossible to measure. Such influence is exercised over U.S. Middle East policy by the Israeli lobby in the U.S.

125. ibid., p. 12.

126. Lester, W. Milbrath, "Interest Groups and Foreign Policy," Domestic Sources of Foreign Policy, (New York, James N. Rosenau (ed.) The Free Press, 1966), p. 231

127. Howard E. Freeman and Moms Showel, "Differential Political Influence of Voluntary Associations," Public Opinion Quarterly, Winter 1951-52, p. 703

128. F. Chiedozie Ogene, Interest Groups and the Shaping of Foreign Policy, (2nd Edition), (New York, St. Martin's Press, 1983), p.1.

129. ibid., p. 295.

130. ibid.

131. ibid., p. 196

132. Harold Sprout and Margaret Sprout, "Environmental Factors in the Study of International Politics" in Harold Karan Jacobson and William Zimmerman, The Shaping of Foreign Policy, (New York, Atherton Press, 1969), p.45.

133. Vernon McKay, Southern African and Its Implication for American Policy," William A. Hance (ed.), Southern Africa and the U.S., (New York, Columbia University Press, 1968), p. 3.

134. For opposing views of U.S. strategic interest in Southern Africa, see A.J. Gottrell and R.M. Burnell, "The Soviet Navy and the Indian Ocean," Strategic Review, 2, No. 4, Fall 1974, and Michael T. Klare, "Superpower Rivalry at Sea," Foreign Policy, 21, (Winter 1975-1976).

135. Herschell Sullivan Challenor, "The Influence of Black Americans on U.S. Foreign Policy Toward Africa" in Abdul Aziz Said (ed), Ethnicity and U.S. Foreign Policy, (New York, Praegen Publishers, 1981), p. 143.

136. ibid., p. 144.

137. ibid., p. 159

138. ibid., p. 175

139. Ronald W. Walters, "African-American Influence on U.S. Foreign Policy Toward South Africa," in Mohammed E. Ahrari, (ed), Ethnic Groups and U.S. Foreign Policy, (New York, Greenwood Press, 1987), p. 66.

140. ibid., p. 79.

141. Kevin Danaher, In Whose Interest, (Washington, D.C., Institute for Policy Studies, 1984), p. 2.

142. Paul Deats, "U.S. Religious Institutions and South Africa" Alfred Hero, Jr. and John Barrat (eds), The American People and Southern Africa, (Indiana, Lexington Press, 1981).

143. John Wright, "Contributions, lobbying, and committee voting in the U.S. House of Representatives," APSR, June 1990, Vol. 84, No. 2, p. 425.

144. Harold D. Lasswell and Abraham Kaplan, Power and Society, (London, Rutledge and Kegan Paul, Ltd., 1952), p. 71.

145. Nader Saiedi, "What is Islamic Fundamentalism?" in J. Jeffrey, P. Hadden and Anson Shupe (eds), Prophetic Religions and World Politics, New York, Paragon House Publishers, 1986, pp. 173-193.

146. Roland Robertson, "Liberation Theology in Latin America: Sociological Problems of Interpretation and Explanation," ibid., pp. 73-100.

147. Theodore A. Couloumbis and James H. Wolfe, Introduction to International Relations (3rd edition), Prentice-Hall, Inc., Englewood Cliffs, New Jersey, 1986, p. 384.

148. Contrary to historical evidence, some African American groups have often condemned European/Christian colonization of Africa while totally ignoring Arab/Moslem colonization, which proceeded the former by many centuries.

149. The New American Bible, (New York, Catholic Book Publishing Co., 1970), p. 826.

150. Constant H. Jacquet, Jr. and Alice M. Jones (eds.), 1991 Yearbook of American and Canadian Churches, (Nashville, Abingdon Press, 1991), p. 270.

151. Frank S. Mead and Samuel S. Hill, Handbook of Denominations in the U.S. (9th edition), (Nashville, Abingdon Press, 1985), p. 221.

152. Jacquet and Jones (eds), op.cit, idem.

153. The Washington Post, Parade Magazine, April 5, 1991, p. 2. In per capita income, the Mormons are the richest with over $8 billion in real estate, radio, etc.

154. Hana, op. cit., p. 27.

155. "Documentation for the General Meeting of the NCCB and USCC, Action Item, No. 15, November 14, 1991," pp. 485-521.

156. ibid.

157. "Network, A Voice in Washington for Social Justice, A Brochure of the Network Lobby." p. 2.

158. Interview with Sr. Pinkerton, op. cit.

159. Network, op. cit.

160. ibid.

161. Kit and Frederica Konolidge, The Power of Their Glory, America's Ruling Class: The Episcopalians, (New York, Wyden Books, 1978), Lp. 27.

162. ibid., p. 105.

163. ibid., p. 7.

164. "The Episcopal Church Washington Office," A Bulletin of the Episcopal Church.

165. "Mission Statement of the WOA," January 28, 1992.

166. Jacquet and Jones (ed) op. cit. idem.

167. ibid.

168. United Church of Christ, History and Program, (New York, United Church Press, 1982), p. 58.

169. ibid.

170. Frank S. Mead and Samuel S. Hill, Handbook of Denominations in the U.S., (9th edition), (Nashville, Abingdon Press, 1985), p. 164.

171. Jacquet and Jones (eds.) op. cit., p. 271.

172. ibid., p. 276.

173. Mead and Hill, op. cit., p. 168.

174. Menendes, op. cit., p. 3.

175. Wellington W. Nyangoni, African Nationalism in Zimbabwe (Rhodesia, (Washington, D.C., University Press of America, 1977), p. 1.

176. Ibid. Rasmussen places the date of Matabele migration from South Africa to Zimbabwe between 1838 to 1839. See R. Kent Rasmussen, Migrant Kingdom, Mzilikazi's Ndebele in South Africa, (London: Rex Collings Ltd., 1978), p. 133.

177. A.J. Wills, An Introduction to the History of Central Africa, (London, Oxford University Press, 1964), p. 23.

178. Basil Davidson, A History of East and Central Africa to the Late Nineteenth Century, (New York, Doubleday and Co., Inc. 1969), p. 270.

179. ibid.

180. John G. Jackson, Introduction to African Civilizations, (Secausus, N.J., 1970), p. 33.

181. Jackson, op cit. p. 31.

182. ibid. p. 33. This writer is proud to come from the same village as King Jaja, where his legendary feats are still celebrated in songs, stories, and festivals.

183. ibid. p. 7.

184. Larry Brown, Politics in Rhodesia, (Boston, Harvard University Press, 1973), p. 8.

185. Frank Clements, Rhodesia: A Study of The Deterioration of a White

Society, (New York, Frederick A. Praeger, 1969), pp. 8-9.

186. T.R.M. Creighton, The Anatomy of Partnership: Southern Rhodesia and the Central African Federation, (London, Faber and Faber, Ltd., 1960), p. 25.

187. Stafford Glass, Matabele War, (London, Longmans Green and Co. Ltd., 1968), p. 5.

188. B. Vulindkela Mtshali, Rhodesia: Background to Conflict, (New York, . Hawthorn Books, Inc., 1967), p. 31.

189. Hugh Marshall Hole, Lobengula, (London, Philip Alan and Co., Ltd., 1929), p. 134.

190. T.O. Ranger, Revolt in Southern Rhodesia, 1896-7, (London, Heinemann Educational Books Ltd., 1967), p. 217.

191. Brown, op cit.

192. Jackson, op. cit., p. 31.

193. Ranger, op. cit., p. 217.

194. ibid.

195. From Bishop of Mashonoland to CNC, 25 February, 1903, All/2/18/3 in Nyangoni, op. cit., p. 38.

196. ibid.

197. T.O. Ranger, The African Voice in Southern Africa, (London, Heinemann Educational Books, 1970), pp. 10-11.

198. Nyangoni, op. cit., p. 36.

199. ibid.

200. ibid.

201. ibid., p. 37.

202. Ranger, op. cit., p. 321.

203. Nyangoni, op. cit., p. 38.

204. Nathan Shamuyarira, Crisis in Rhodesia, (London, Andre Deutsch Ltd., 1965), pp. 28-29.

205. Nyangoni, op. cit., p. 46.

206. Ndabaningi Sithole, African Nationalism, (New York, Oxford University Press, 1959), p. 57.

207. The Federation of the Rhodesias and Nyasaland consisted of present day Zimbabwe, Zambia and Malawi. An attempt at "multi-racial politics" in Africa, it was formed in 1957 with the blessing of the British but collapsed in 1963. Even though the overwhelming majority of the Federation was white, its prime minister, Sir Roy Welensky, was a white settler from Zimbabwe.

208. Ian Linden, The Catholic Church and the Struggle for Zimbabwe, (London, Longmon Group Limited, 1980), p. 61.

209. Nyangoni, op. cit., p. 47.

210. ibid., p. 141.

211. ibid.

212. ibid.

213. Colin Stoneman (ed), Zimbabwe's Inheritance, (New York, St. Martin's Press, 1981), p. 24.

214. Robert C. Good, UDI, The International Politics of Rhodesian Rebellion, (Princeton, N.J., Princeton University Press, 1973), p. 1.

215. Harold Wilson, A Personal Record: The Labour Government 1964-1970, (New York, The Atlantic Monthly Press, 1971), p. 178.

216. Good, op. cit., p. 103.

217. ibid.

218. British Government Factel, No. 577, p. 5.

219. ibid., p. 6.

220. David Lan, Gun and Rain, Guerrillas and Spirit Mediums in

Zimbabwe, (Berkeley, University of California Press), p. 124.

221. ibid., pp. 6-7.

222. Theodore Bull, Rhodesia, Crisis in Color, (Chicago, Quadrangle Books Inc., 1967), p. 16.

223. This writer found this song in an unaccredited one-page bulletin.

224. Anthony Lake, The "Tar Baby" Option, (New York, Columbia University Press, 1976), p. 199.

225. ibid.

226. ibid.

227. For the official texts of the relevant bills and resolutions - S 1404, HR45, H.J.R. 172, 423, and H. Cong. Res. 5,6,12,21 of 1971 Congressional Record.

228. Lake, op. cit., p. 213.

229. ibid., p. 217.

230. ibid., p. 218.

231. Vernon McKay, "The Domino Theory of the Rhodesian Lobby," Africa Report, XII: 6 (June 1966), p. 57.

232. Lake, op. cit., p. 231.

233. Ogene, op. cit., p. 190.

234. Lake, ibid.

235. Committee on Foreign Relations, United States Senate, "Importation of Rhodesian Chrome," September 6, 1973, p. 88.

236. Lake, op. cit., p. 230.

237. Ogene, op. cit., p. 210.

238. Lake, op. cit., pp. 226.227.

239. ibid., pp. 232-233.

240. ibid.

241. Lake, op. cit., p. 270.

242. ibid.

243. ibid., p. 272.

244. ibid., p. 274.

245. ibid., p. 275.

246. WNA, Spring 1977, pp. 3-4.

247. ibid. p. 4.

248. ibid.

249. WNA, October, 1975, p. 1.

250. ibid.

251. ibid. p. 2.

252. ibid. pp. 2-3.

253. WNA, Summer 1978, p.4.

254. Lake, op. cit., p. 235.

255. Interview with Rev. Ted Lockwood, Washington, D.C.,
     February 2, 1991.

256. Jeffrey M. Berry, The Interest Group Society, (Boston, Little, Brown and
     Company, 1984), p. 116.

257. ibid.

258. Tip O'Neal, Man of the House, (New York, St. Martin's Press, 1987),
     p. 388.

259. Interview with Rev. Ted Lockwood, op. cit.

260. "United Methodist Information, The General News Service of theUnited Methodist Church," New York, May 9, 1975, p.1.

261. "United Methodist Information, The General News Service of the United Methodist Church, (New York, December 10, 1975), p. 1.

262. ibid., p. 2.

263. "Social Policy Statements and Recommended Actions, A Publication of the United Methodist Church," December 1988, p. 180.

264. ibid.

265. General Board of Church and Society, The National Methodist Church, September 1989 for the 1989-1992 quadrennium, p. 4.

266. ibid., p. 6.

267. ibid., p. 6

268. Will, op. cit., p. 236.

269. Walter J. Oleszek, Congressional Procedures and the Policy Process, (Washington, D.C., Congressional Quarterly Inc., 1978), p. 70.

270. Juspax, August 1987, Vol. 7, No. 3, p. 2.

271. Origins, September 23, 1976, Vol. 6, No. 14, pp. 211-215.

272. Origins, June 6, 1974, Vol. 4, No. 2, p. 25.

273. "UN Sanctions Against Rhodesia," USCC Congressional Testimony, Fall 1973, p. 1.

274. ibid., p. 2.

275. Pope John XXIII, "Pacem in Terris" (n 143), 1963.

276. U.S. 95th Congress, Hearings Senate Committee on Foreign Relations, p. 2.

277. U.S. 95th Congress Hearings, House Committee on International Relations, p. 25.

278. ibid., p. 26.

279. James S. Rausch, "Open-Letter to Henry Kissinger," April 7, 1976, p. 3.

280. ibid.

281. Rev. Interview with Rev. Ted Lockwood, Washington, D.C., February 14, 1991.

282. Linden, op. cit., p. 208.

283. ibid., p. 209.

284. Sojourners, April 1986, p. 6.

285. John Marcum, The Angolan Revolution: Cambridge, Massachusetts;1969, p.1

286.   ibid.

287.   ibid.

288. David Birminham, The Portuguese Conquest of Angola: The Mbundu and Their Neighbors Under the Influence of the Portuguese, 1483-1790 (Oxford: Clarendon Press, 1966), p.89.

289. ibid. pp. 9-10.

290.   ibid. p. 10

291. David Birmingham, Trade and Conflict in Angola: The Mbundu and Their Neighbors Under the Influence of the Portuguese 1483-1790, (Oxford, Clarendon Press, 1966), p. 89.

292. Marcum, op. cit., pp. 21-22.

293.   George Padmore, PanAfricanism or Communism, The Coming
                   Struggle for Africa (New York: Roy Publishers, 1956), p. 141.

294. 298

295. ibid., p. 27.

296. Arthur Maciel, <u>Angola Heroica.</u> (Lisbon: Livraria Bertrand, 1963), p. 67.

297. Marcum, <u>op. cit.</u>, p. 30.

298. Basil Davidson, <u>Angola, 1961: The Factual Record</u> (London: Union of Democratic Control, 1962), p. 6.

299. <u>ibid. p. 53.</u>

300. <u>ibid.</u>p. 58.

301. Holden Roberto eventually became the leader of the U.S.-backed National Front fot the Liberation of Angola (FNLA), which lost to MPLA during the Angolan civil war.

302. Marcum, <u>op. cit.</u> pp. 61-62.

303. <u>ibid., p. 68.</u>

304. <u>ibid.</u> p. 110.

305. <u>ibid.</u>, pp. 124-125.

306. <u>ibid.</u>, p. 125.

307. Le Master, "Horror in Angola", <u>Time</u>, February 24, 1961, p. 54.

308. Confidential Interviews, 8, and 23 (A staff of the National Security Council and CIA officer serving under Bronson Tweedy in the Africa Division).

309. Henry F. Jackson, <u>op. cit.</u>, p. 57.

310. <u>New York Times,</u> May 21, 1960. <u>Department of State Bulletin,</u> June 6, 1960.

311. Report on the United Nations: 1961, pp. 48-49.

312. <u>ibid., p. 58.</u>

313. <u>ibid.</u>

314. George M. Houser, "The Rebellion in Angola," <u>Concern,</u> (Washington:

Board of Christian Social Concerns of the Methodist Church), Vol. 4, No. 13, July 1, 1962, pp. 3-6.

315. Herman Will, A Will for Peace, (Washington, D.C., The General Board of Church and Society of the United Methodist Church, 1984), p. 233.

316. ibid.

317. ibid.

318. Concern, December 1, 1961, p. 17.

319. Don Teodosio Clemente de Gouvera, (The Voice of the Pastor, Lisbon, 1961), pp. 14-15.

320. "Angola, Secret Government, Documents on Counter-Subversion," Translated and edited by Caroline Reuver-Cohen and William Jerman, New York, 1 document, 1974, pp. 171-172.

321. Serapiao, op. cit., p. 328.

322. Interview with Dr. Stan Ani, Washington, D.C., August 1991.

323. Lorene K. Fox (ed), East African Childhood, (London, Oxford University Press, 1967), p. 125.

324. C.A.I.P. News, Vol. XXVIII, No. 4, April 1967, p. 2.

325. Jackson, op. cit., p. 170.

326. Washington Notes on Africa, Summer 1980, p. 5.

327. Pat O'Connor et al., Washington, D.C., Congressional Quarterly Inc., p. 878.

328. Presidential Documents, Vol. II, No. 5, Monday, December 22, 1975, p. 1383.

329. Department of State Bulletin, Vol. LXXIV, No. 1912, February 16, 1976, p. 175.

330. Legislation on Foreign Relations Through 1978, Vol. I, U.S. Senate and U.S. House of Representatives, February 1979, p. 293.

331. Ronald W. Walters, "The Clark Amendment: An Analysis of U.S. Policy

Choices in Angola", The Black Scholar, Vol. 12, No. 4, July-August 1981, p. 5.

332. ibid., p. 4.

333. ibid.

334. Gerald Bender, "Kissinger in Angola: Anatomy of Failure" in Rene Lemarchand (ed.) American Policy in Southern Africa: The Stakes and the Stance, (Washington, D.C. University Press of America, 1978), p. 85.

335. ibid, p. 85.

336. ibid., p. 98.

337. ibid., p. 99.

338. Leslie H. Gelb, "U.S. Aides Tell Senators of Arms Aid to Angolans," The New York Times, November 7, 1975, The Washington Post, November 8, 1975.

339. Bender, op. cit., p. 102.

340. Washington Notes on Africa, March 29, 1976, p. 6.

341. ibid.

342. ibid., p. 7.

343. ibid., p. 8.

344. Gerald J. Bender, "Testimony on U.S. Angolan Policy," May 25, 1978, p. 2.

345. ibid.

346. ibid.

347. Washington Notes on Africa, Summer 1980, p. 6.

348. ibid., p. 5.

349. ibid.

350. ibid. p. 6.

351. Washington Notes on Africa, Winter 80/81, p. 3.

352. ibid.

353. ibid. p. 6.

354. Washington Notes on Africa, Winter 1984, p. 5.

355. Rothchild and Ravenhill, op. cit., p. 408.

356. Washington Notes on Africa, Summer 1985, p. 7.

357. ibid.

358. Cherri Waters, "Destabilizing Angola: South Africa's War and U.S. Policy," Washington Office on Africa Educational Fund   and Center for International Policy, December 1986, p. 9. ct also Rothchild and Ravenhill, ibid.

359. ibid.

360. The Washington Post, February 3, 1986, p. A1.

361. Margaret A. Novicki, Africa Report, July-August 1986, pp. 35-41.

362. Washington Notes on Africa, Fall 1985, p.1.

363. Waters, op. cit., p. 7.

364. Washington Notes on Africa, op. cit.

365. ibid. p. 2.

366. Theodore J. Lowi, "Making Democracy Safe for the World: National Politics and Foreign Policy" in Rosenau, op. cit., p. 300.

367. Gann and Duignan, op. cit. p. 69.

368. Robert E. DiClerico, The American Presidency (Englewood Cliffs, N.J., Prentice-Hall, Inc., 1979), p. 33.

369. "Interview with Ted Lockwood", Washington, D.C., February 18, 1991.

370. ibid.

371. ibid.

372. New York Times, December 19, 1975. p.1. It was also Hersch who broke the news on the My Lai massacre in Vietnam in 1972.

373. Howard Wolpe, "Seizing Southern African Opportunities," Foreign Policy, No. 73, Winter 1988-89, pp. 63-64.

374. Washington Notes on Africa, op. cit., p. 2.

375. ibid.

376. ibid.

377. ibid.

378. Gretchen Eick, "To Aid Unita: The Churches in Angola Speak," A pamphlet of the U.C.C., November 11, 1985, p. 2.

379. ibid.

380. ibid.

381. ibid.

382. Lawrence Henderson, "Letter from Angola," January 19, 1986.

383. ibid.

384. "Interview with Gretchen Eick," Washington, D.C., February 15, 1991.

385. Juspax,Vol. 7., No.3, August 1987, p. 1.

386. ibid.

387. Gretchen Eick, "To Aid UNITA? The Churches in Angola Speak," A Pamphlet of U.C.C., November 11, 1985, p. 2.

388. "Statement on Portuguese Violations or Human Rights in Its African Territories," March 19-20, 1974, p. 1.

389. ibid.

390. ibid., p. 3.

391. Network, A Catholic Social Justice Lobby, no date or page.

392. "Interview with Sr. Catherine Pinkerton," C.S.J., March 11, 1991.

393. ibid.

394. ibid.

395. ibid.

396. Hugh Hecto, "Issue Networks and the Executive Establishment," in Anthony King, ed., The New American Politically System, Washington, D.C., American Enterprise Institute, 1978, pp. 87-124. See also Robert w. Kweit and Mary Griesez Kweit, "Bureaucratic Decision-Making: Impediments to Citizen Participation," Polity 12, Summer 1980, pp. 647-666.

397. Network, Vol. 14, No. 6, November-December, p. 9.

398. Lockwood, op. cit., p. 114.

399. Mohammed E. El-Khawas and Barry Cohen (eds.), The Kissinger Study of Southern Africa, (Westport, Connecticut, Lawrence Hill and Col, 1976), pp. 105-106.

400. Rausch, op. cit., p. 1.

401. ibid., p. 2.

402. "Interview with Fr. Rawlings Lambert", Washington, D.C., March 1990.

403. Henderson, op. cit., p. 3.

404. Alexander Dallin and Gail W. Lapidus, "Reagan and the Russians: American Policy Toward the Soviet Union," in Oye et al, Eagle Resurgent, The Reagan Era in American Foreign Policy, Boston, Little, Brown and Col, 1987, p. 1983.

405. Reagan's State of the Union Message as reprinted in the New York Times, January 27, 1982, p. 8.

406. Donald Rothchild and John Ravenhill, "Subordinating African Issues to Global Logic: Reagan Confronts Political Complexity" in Oye et al., op.

cit., p. 403.

407. Dallin and Lapidus, op. cit., p. 207.

408. James V. D'Amato, "Constructive Engagement: The Rise and Fall of an American Foreign Policy," Ph.D. Dissertation,   University of South Carolina, 1986, p. 313.

409. Ronald Walters, "Beyond Sanctions: A comprehensive U.S. Policy for Southern Africa," World Policy Journal, Winter 1986-1987, p. 92.

410. Crocker's position was stated in several articles including, "Lost in Africa," New Republic, February 18, 1978, pp. 15-17, "Missing Opportunities in Africa," co-authored with W.H. Lewis, Foreign Policy, Summer, 1979, pp. 10-13.

411. D'Amato, op. cit., p. 95.

412. ibid., p. 96.

413. Chester A. Crocker, "South Africa: A Strategy for Change," Foreign Affairs, Winter 1980/1981, p. 345.

414. William Minter, "Destructive Engagement: The U.S. and South Africa in the Reagan Era," in Johnson and Martin (eds.), Destructive Engagement, (Zimbabwe, Zimbabwe Publishing House, 1986), p. 292.

415. Danaher, op. cit., p. 5.

416. Transcript of televised interview, "A Conversation with the President," CBS News Special Report with Walter Cronkite, March 3, 1981, p. 8.

417. Jackson, op. cit., p. 236.

418. ibid., p. 279.

419. ibid., p. 280.

420. Johnson and Martin, op. cit., p. 300.

421. ibid., p. 300.

422. Jackson, op. cit., p. 236.

423. ibid.

424. Johnson and Martin, op. cit., p. 300.

425. ibid.

426. Legislation on Foreign Relations, 1983-84, p. 1.

427. Legislation on Foreign Relations, 1984-'85, p. 1.

428. Staff Report for the Committee on the District of Columbia, House of Representatives, 99th Congress, April 26, 11984, p. v.

429. Legislation on Foreign Policy, 1984-'85, pp. 1-2.

430. WNA, Autumn 1983, p. 1.

431. ibid.

432. ibid.

433. ibid., p. 2.

434. ibid.

435. ibid., p. 4.

436. ibid.

437. James North, Freedom Rising, (New York, New American Library, 1986), p. 330.

438. ibid.

439. Stuart Jackson, "Business Week/Harris Poll: Fight Apartheid, But Don't Close Up Shop," Business Week, February 11, 1985, p. 39.

440. John Hanlon and Roger Omond, The Sanctions Handbook, (New York, Viking Penguin, 1987), P. 178.

441. ibid.

442. ibid.

443. Congressional Quarterly, October 4, 1986, p. 2340.

444. Donald Rothchild and John Ravenhill, "Subordinating African Issues to Global Logic: Reagan Confronts Political Complexity," in Oye, Lieber et al., Eagle Resurgent, (Boston, Little, Brown and Col, 1987), p. 411.

445. 1985 Almanac, p. 83.

446. WNA, Spring 1986, p. 1.

447. ibid., p. 2.

448. Congressional Quarterly, op. cit., p. 2341.

449. ibid.

450. ibid.

451. Congressional Quarterly Almanac, Vol. XLII, 1986, p.   359.

452. The two others are: (1) In 1973, Congress overrode Nixon's veto and enacted the War Powers Resolution, which gave it the right to withdraw U.S. troops from combat (cf. 1973 Congressional Quarterly Almanac, pp. 90-95), (2) In the mid 1970's, congress forced Ford to accept two major foreign bills he vetoed: (a) embargo on arms sales to Turkey (1974), (b) a bill giving Congress the right to veto foreign arms sales (cf. 1974 Q. Almanac, p. 547 and the 1976 Q. Almanac, p. 213.

453. Congressional Quarterly Almanac, op. cit., p. 359.

454. Patrice Gaines-Carter, "Triumphant Moment for TransAfrica, Sanctions Approval Elates Lobbyists," The Washington Post, Saturday, October 4, 1986, p. A16.

455. Edgar Lockwood, South Africa's Moment of Truth, (New York, Friendship Press, 1988), p. 45.

456. ibid.

457. ibid., p. 42.

458. Deats, op. cit., p. 104.

459. ibid., p. 103.

460. Neville Richardson, "Apartheid, heresy and the Church in South Africa," The Journal of Religious Ethics, Vol. 14, No. 1, Spring 1986, p. 5.

461. Juspax, op. cit., p. 3.

462. ibid.

463. ibid.

464. Juspax, op. cit., p.2.

465. ibid.

466. ibid.

467. ibid., p. 2.

468. ibid., p. 2.

469. "Divestment, Disinvestment and South Africa: A Policy Statement, Administrative Board of The United States Catholic Conference," p. 2.

470. Albert Luthuli, Let My People Go: The Autobiography of a Great African Leader, (Johannesburg, Collins, 1962), p. 209.

471. INFO: SA, and SACBC News Service, Vol. 2, No. 9, May 11, 1987, pp. 1-2.

472.   USCC, "Letter to Senate Foreign Relations Committee," June 10, 1988, p. 2.

473.   Origins, February 19, 1987, Vol. 16, No. 36, p. 636.

474.   "Statement on South Africa By USCC Administrative Board," op. cit., p.5.

475.   WNA, Winter/Spring, op. cit., p. 7.

476.   ibid.

477.   "Statement on South Africa By USCC," op. cit., p. 5.

478.   U.S.C.C., "Letter to Senate Foreign Relations Committee," op. cit., ibid.

479. "Confidential Interview", Washington, D.C., March 30, 1992.

480. ibid.

481.   "Network Legislative Seminar XVII Briefing Sheet:
     South Africa."

482.   Network, Vol. 14, No. 6, op. cit., ibid.

483.   ibid.

484.   "Interview with Sr. Pinkerton," op. cit.

485.   Network, op. cit.

486.   "Memo to the United States Senate Foreign Relations
     Committee,"   June 1985, p. 1.

487.   ibid.

488.   Philip Deemer (ed.), Episcopal Year, Vol. 2., (New
     York, Jarrow Press,   Inc., 1970), p. 13.

489.   ibid.

490. ibid.

491.   ibid., pp. 13-14.

492.   ibid., p. 14.

493. ibid., p. 14.

494.   Episcopal Diocese of Washington, 1986 Journal and
     Directory, p. 165.

495.   "Interview With Canon Kwasi Thornell", Washington,
     D.C., April 15,   1992.

496.   "Confidential Interview", Washington, D.C., March
     17,   1992"

497.   ibid.

498.   ibid.

499.   ibid.

500.   This does not mean that the Episcopal/Anglican
Church is a white   .   .
                church. It is not. The overwhelming majority of
members of the Anglican
                Communion are non-white.   However,inboth
the U.S. and South Africa,
                the upper echelons of the clergy are white.

501.   William Johnston, "South African Church Stirs Pot,"
Witness, January
                1986, p. 6.

502.   ibid.

503.   WNA Winter/Spring 1985, op. cit., p. 8/

504.   ibid.

505.   ibid.

506.   ibid.

507.   "Interview with Fr. Nathaniel Porter." Rev. Porter has
close relations
                with Tutu. He supervised his visits to the Washington,
D.C. area and
                acted as guardian for Tutu's daughter, Mpho, a
graduate of the Howard
                University School of Engineering.

508. "Report to the Eleventh General Synod of the United Church of Christ on
   1975-1977 Corporate Social Responsibility Actions, With Special
   Emphasis on Southern Africa," p. 1.

509. ibid.

510. ibid., p. 2.

511. ibid., p. 18.

512. ibid.

513. ibid., p. 25.

514. ibid.

515. U.C.C. Network, October, 1985, Vol. 8, No. 8, p. 1.

516. "Interview with U.C.C. Staff", Washington, D.C., February 15, 1991.

517. ibid.

518. ibid.

519. Dorothy, Dohen, Nationalism and American Catholicism, (New York, Sheed and Ward, 1968), p. 1.

520. James Hennesey, American Catholics, (Oxford, Oxford University Press, 1981), pp. 266-268.

521. Madonna Kolberschlag (ed), Between God and Caesar, Priests, Sisters, and Political Office in the U.S., New York, Paulist Press, 1985, P. 142.

522. Oleszek, op. cit., p. 35.

523. ibid.

524. James Adams, The Growing Church Lobby in Washington, (Grand Rapids, MI, Eerdmans, 1970), p. 231.

525. Clark E. Cochran, "Public/Private - Secular/Sacred: A Context for Understanding the Church-State Debate," Journal of Church and State, Vol. 29, 1987, p. 116. See also Michael Waltzer, "Liberalism and the Art of Separation," Political Theory, 12 (August 1987).

526. UCC Network, January 1981, Vol. 4, No. 1, P. 1.

527. ibid.

528. Time, December 9, 1991, p. 63.

529. Code of Canon Law, (Vatican City, Liberia Editrice Vaticana, 1983), p. 103.

530. Nigeria News, From the Embassy of Nigeria, Vol. 1, Issue 3, January 1992, p. 1.

531. This writer was once asked by his people to serve on the town council. But when he asked for the bishop's permission, he was rebuffed.

532. "Confidential - Interview," Washington, D.C., April 1992. In fact the Vatican is one of the few countries that have recognized the military junta in Port au Prince.

533. Robert H. Jackson and Carl G. Rosberg, Personal Rule in Black Africa, (Berkeley, University of California Press, 1982), p. 89.

534. Archbishop Denis Hurley, "South Africa: Its Immovable Object and Irresistible Force," Origins, February 19, 1987, Vol. 16., No. 36, p. 635.

535. ibid.

536. ibid.

537. Lynn Rosselini, "Lobbyists' Row All Alert for Chance at the Budget," The New York Times, February 26, 1981 in Berry, op. cit., p. 17.

538. Walt Harrington, "The Education of David Carmen," The Washington Post Magazine, February 28, 1988, p. 15.

539. Hedrick Smith, The Power Game, How Washington Works, (New York, Ballantine Books, 1988), p. 217.

540. ibid., p. 233.

541. "Interview with Sister Catherine Pinkerton, CSSJ", Washington, D.C., March 11, 1992.

542. "Interview with Rev. Robert Brooks" Washington, D.C., February 1992.

543. Muzorewa lost his credibility after he allied himself with Ian Smith.

SELECTED BIBLIOGRAPHY

BOOKS

Ahran, Mohammed E. (ed). Ethnic Groups and U.S. Foreign   Policy. New York: Greenwood Press, 1987.

Ali, Sheik R. Southern Africa, An American Enigma. New   York: Praeger, 1987.

Almond, Gabriel A. The American People and Foreign Policy. New York: Frederick A. Praeger, 1960.

Aziz, Abdul (ed). Ethnicity and Foreign Policy, New York: Praeger Publisher, 1981.

Berry, Jeffrey, M. The Interest Group Society. Boston: Little, Brown and Col, 1984.

Brown, Larry. Politics in Rhodesia. Boston: Harvard University Press, 1973.

Bull, Theodore, Rhodesia, Crisis in Color. Chicago: Quadrangle Books Inc., 1967.

Caraley, D. and Epstein, M. (eds). The Making of American   Foreign and Domestic Policy. New York:

General Health Publishing Corp., 1978.

Carter, G.M. and O'Meara, P. (eds). International Politics   in
Southern Africa. Bloomington: Indiana University Press, 1982.

Chirenje, M.J. Ethiopianism and Afro-American in South   Africa.
LSU Press, 1987.

Clements, Frank. Rhodesia: A Study of the Deterioration of   a White
Society. New York: Frederick A. Praeger, 1969.

Cohen, Bernard C. The Influence of Non-Governmental Groups
        in Foreign Policy Making. Boston: World Peace Foundation,
1959.

Couloumbis, Theodore A. and Wolfe, James A. Introduction to
International Relations. Prentice-Hall Inc., Englewood Cliffs, New
Jersey, 1986.

Creighton, T.R.M. The Anatomy of Partnership: Southern   Rhodesia
and the Central African Federation. London: Faber and Faber Ltd., 1960.

Dahl, Robert A. Congress and Foreign Policy. New York:
Harcourt, Brace and Co., 1950.

Danaher, Kevin. In Whose Interest? Washington, D.C.:   Institute
for Policy Studies, 1984.

David, Ian. Gun and Rain, Guerrillas and Spirit Mediums in
Zimbabwe. Berkeley: University of California Press, 1980.

Davidson, Basil. A History of East and Central Africa to   the Late
Nineteenth Century. New York: Doubleday and Co., Inc., 1969.

Dohen, Doherty, Nationalism and American Catholicism. New   York:
Sheed and Ward, 1968.

Emerson, Rupert. Africa and United States Policy.   Englewood Cliffs,
N.J.: Prentice Hall Inc., 1967.

Fox, Lorene K. (ed). East African Childhood. London: Oxford
University Press, 1967.

Glass, S. Matabele War. London: Longmans, Green and Co.   Ltd.,
1968.

Glendenen, Clarence, et al. Americans in Africa, 1865-1900.   Stanford,
California: Stanford University, 1964.

Good, Robert C. UDI, The International Politics of   Rhodesian
Rebellion. Princeton, N.J.: Princeton University Press, 1973.

Hamilton, M.P. (ed). American Character and Foreign Policy.   Grand
Rapids, Michigan: William B. Earlmans Publishing Co., 1986.

Hance, William (ed). Southern Africa and the United States.   New
York: Columbia University Press, 1968.

Hanlon, John and Ormond, Roger. The Sanctions Handbook.   New
                                                          York:
Viking Penguin, 1987.

Hanna, Mary. Catholics and American Politics. Cambridge,
Massachusetts: Harvard University Press, 1979.

Harrick, David. Two Decades of debate: The Controversy   Over
U.S. Companies in South Africa. Washington, D.C.: Investor
Responsibility Research Center, 1983.

Hennesey, James. American Catholics. Oxford: Oxford
University Press, 1981.

Hero, Alfred and Barrats (eds), The American People and   South
Africa. Indiana: Lexington Press, 1981.

Hole, Hugh M. Lobengula. London: Philip Alan and Co.   Ltd.,
                                                      1929.

Irish, M.D. et al. Readings in the Politics of American Democracy.
Englewood Cliffs, N.J.: Prentice Hall Inc., 1965.

Jackson, Henry F. From the Congo to Soweto, U.S. Foreign   Policy Toward Africa Since 1960. New York: New York Quill, 1984.

Jackson, John G. Introduction to African Civilizations.   N.J.: Secaucus, 1970.

Jackson, Phyllis and Martin, David (eds). Destructive Engagement. Harare: Zimbabwe Publishing House, 1986.

Jacobs, Sylvia M. (ed). Black Americans and the Missionary Movement in Africa. Westport, Connecticut, 1982.

Jacobson, Harold K. and Zimmerman, William (eds). The   Shaping of Foreign Policy. New York: Atherton Press, 1969.

Jeffrey, J. et al. Prophetic Religions and World Politics.   New York: Paragon House Publishers, 1986.

Key, V.O. Public Opinion and American Democracy. New York: Alfred Knopf, 1961.

Khawas, M.E. and Cohen, Barry (eds). The Kissinger Study of Southern Africa. Westport, Connecticut, 1982.

King, A. (ed). The New American Political System. Washington, D.C.: American Enterprise Institute, 1978.

Kolberschlag, Madonna. Between God and Caesar, Priests,   Sisters and Political Office in the U.S.. New York: Paulist Press, 1985.

Lake, Anthony. The "Tar Baby" Option. New York, Columbia University Press, 1976.

Laski, Harold J. The American Democracy. New York: the   Viking Press, 1948.

Lasswell, Harold D. and Kaplan, Abraham. Power and Society. New Haven: Connecticut University Press, 1950.

Lemarchand, Rene (ed). <u>American Policy in Southern Africa</u>.
Washington, D.C.: University Press of America Inc., 1978.
Linden, Ian. <u>The Catholic Church and the Struggle for</u>
<u>Zimbabwe</u>. London: Longmans Group Ltd., 1980.

Lockwood, Edgar. <u>South Africa's Moment of Truth</u>. New York:
      Friendship Press, 1988.

Love, J. <u>The U.S. Anti-Apartheid Movement</u>. New York: Praeger,
1985.

Luthuli, Albert. <u>Let My People Go: The Autobiography of A</u>   <u>Great</u>
<u>African Leader</u>. Johannesburg: Collins, 1962.

Mazrui, Ali A. <u>Africa's International Relations</u>. Boulder,
Colorado: Westview Press, 1979.

Morgenthau, Hans J. <u>Politics Among Nations</u>, 3rd ed. New   York:
Knopf, 1960.

Mtshali, B.V. <u>Rhodesia: Background to Conflict</u>. New York:
Hawthorn Books Inc., 1967.

Mugabane, B.M. <u>The Ties That Bind</u>. Trenton, N.J.: Africa
World Press, 1987.

Nyangoni, Wellington W. <u>African Nationalism</u>. Zimbabwe
(Rhodesia), Washington, D.C.: University Press of America, 1977.

Ogene, F.C. <u>Interest Groups and the Shaping of Foreign</u>   <u>Policy</u>.
New York: St. Martin's Press, 1983.

Oleszek, W.J. Congressional Procedures and the Policy   Process,
Washington, D.C.: Congressional Quarterly Inc., 1978.

Oye, Kenneth A. et al. <u>Eagle Resurgent, The Reagan Era in</u>
<u>American Foreign Policy</u>. Boston: Little, Brown and Co., 1987.

Ranger, T.O. <u>The African Voice in Southern Rhodesia, 1896-</u>   <u>7</u>.

London: Heinemann Educational Books Ltd., 1967.

Regehr, E. Perceptions of Apartheid, The Churches and   Political
Change in South Africa. Scottsdale, Pennsylvania: Herald Press, 1979.

Reichley, A.J. Religion in American Public Life.
Washington, D.C.: The Brookings Institution, 1985.

Rosenau, James (ed) Domestic Sources of Foreign Policy. New   York:
The Free Press, 1966.

Shamuyarira, A. Crisis in Rhodesia. London: Andre Deutsch   Ltd.,
1965.

Shepherd, G.W. Anti-Apartheid, Transitional Conflict and   Western
Policy in the Liberation of South Africa. Westport, Connecticut:
Greenwood Press, 1977.

Sithole, Ndabaninga. African Nationalism. New York: Oxford
University Press, 1959.

Steward, Alexander. The World, the West, and Pretoria. New   York:
David Mckay Co., Inc., 1977.

------The African Voice in Southern Africa. London: Heinemann
Educational Books, 1970.

Welch, C.E. and Meltzer, R. (eds). Human Rights and
Development in Africa. Albany: State University of New York Press,
1984.

-------Who Governs. New Haven: Yale University Press,   1961.

Willan, Brian. "Sol Plaatje," Los Angeles: University of
California Press.

JOURNALS

Adeyemo et al. "How I Wish North American Evangelicals   Would
Influence U.S. Foreign Policy," Transformation, Vol. 2, No. 3,
September 1985.

Baker, R.K. "Toward a New Constituency for a More Active
American Foreign Policy for Africa," Issue, Vol. III,
No. 1, Spring 1973.

Bridgeman, F.B. "The Ethiopian Movement in South Africa,"   The
Missionary Review of the World, June 1984.

Brown, Harold. "The World Council of Churches: Community or
Conspiracy," Fundamentalist Journal, Vol. 2, No. 4, April 1983.

Browning, Ed. "Struggle of Apartheid Not Limited to South   Africa,"
Baptist Witness, 70: 12-15, May 1987.

Cochran, C.E. "Public/Private - Secular/Sacred: A Context   for
Understanding the Church - State Debate," Journal of Church and State,
Vol. 29, 1987.

Crocker, Chester A. "South Africa: A Strategy for Change,"   Foreign
Affairs, Winter, 1980/81.

Freeman, Howard E. and Showell, Morris, "Differential   Political
Influence of Political Associations," Public Opinion Quarterly, Winter,
1951-52.

Jackson, S. "Business Week/Harris Poll: Fight Apartheid,   But
Don't Close Up Shop," Business Week, February 11, 1985.

Johnston, W. "South African Church Stirs Pot," Witness,   January
1986.

-------"Lost in Africa," New Republic, February 18, 1978.

March, James G. "An Introduction to the Theory and   Measurement of

Influence," <u>APSR</u>, Vol. XLIX, (9), No. 2, June 1955.

McKay, V. "The Domino Theory of the Rhodesian Lobby," <u>Africa Report</u>, XII 6 (June 1966).

Menendez, A.J. "Religious Lobbies," <u>Liberty</u>, Vol. 77, No. 2, March-April, 1982.

Minter, William, "South Africa: Straight Talk on Sanctions," <u>Foreign Policy</u>, No. 65, Winter, 1986-87.

-------"Missing Opportunities in Africa," <u>Foreign Policy</u>, Summer, 1979.

Novicki, M.A. <u>Africa Report</u>, July-August 1986.

Serapiao, L.B. "The Preaching of Portuguese Colonialism and the Protest of the White Fathers," <u>Issue</u>, Vol. II, No. 1, Spring 1972.

Skinner, Elliot P. "The Danger of American Support of Apartheid," <u>TransAfrica Forum</u>, No. 1, Vol. 3, Fall 1985.

-------"The Roman Catholic Church and the Principle of Self-Determination," <u>Journal of Church and State</u>, Vol. 23, No. 2, 1981.

Walters, Ronald, "Beyond Sanctions: A Comprehensive U.S. Policy for Southern Africa," <u>World Policy Journal</u>, Winter 1986-1987.

--------"<u>The Black Scholar</u>, Vol. 12, No. 4, July-August 1981.

Waltzer, M. "Liberalism and the Art of Separation," <u>Political Theory</u>, August 12, 1987.

Wright, J. "Contribution, Lobbying, and Committee Voting in the U.S. House of Representatives," <u>APSR</u>, Vol. 84, No. 2, June 1990.

CHURCH DOCUMENTS AND RELATED MATERIALS

Bulletin of the National Catholic Welfare Conference, March 27, 1927, Vol. III.

"C.A.I.P. Statement on Rhodesia," December 1965.

C.A.I.P. News, Vol XXIII, No. 4, March 21, 1967.

Concern, Vol. 4, No. 13, July 1, 1962.

Don Tesdosio Clemente de Gouveia, "The Voice of the Pastor," Lisbon, 1961.

Episcopal Year 1970, Vol. 2, New York, Jarrow Press Inc.
Episcopal Diocese of Washington, 1986 Journal and Directory.

INFO: SA, An SACBC News Service, October 16, 1985.

"Interview with Rev. Rawlings Lambert," Washington, D.C., March 1990.

"Interview with Rev. Edgar Lockwood," Washington, D.C., February 14, 1991.

"Interview with Rev. Edgar Lockwood," Washington, D.C., February 18, 1991.

"Interview with Gretchen Eick," Washington, D.C., February 15, 1991.

"Interview with Gretchen Eick," Washington, D.C., February 22, 1991.

"Interview with Sister Catherine Pinkerton, CSSJ," Washington, D.C., March 11, 1991.

"Confidential Interview," Washington, D.C., March 11, 1991.

"Confidential Interview," Washington, D.C., March 30, 1991.

"Interview with Tom Bailey," Philadelphia, Pa., May 3, 1991.

"Interview with Kenneth Martin," Philadelphia, Pa., May 3, 1991.

"Interview with Jerry Herman," Philadelphia, Pa., May 3,   1991.

"Interview with Rev. Dr. Stan Ani," Washington, D.C., August   1991.

"Interview with L. Robert McClean," Washington, D.C.,
September 9, 1991.

"Interview with Rev. Robert Brooks," Washington, D.C.,   February
1992.

"Confidential Interview," Washington, D.C., March 17, 1992.

"Interview with Rev. Rawlings Lambert," Washington, D.C.,   April
1992.

"Interview with Rev. Nathaniel Porter," Washington, D.C.,   April 6,
1992.

"Interview with Bob Dumas," Washington, D.C., April 1992.

"Interview with Rev. Edgar Lockwood," Washington, D.C.,   April 10,
1992.

"Interview with Canon Kwasi Thornell, Washington, D.C.,   April 15,
1992.

Juspax, Vol. 7, No. 3, August 1987.

"Network Legislative Seminar XVII Briefing Sheet: South   Africa."
Network, Vol. 14, No. 6, November-December, 1986.

Origins, Vol. 4, No. 2, June 6, 1974.

Origins, Vol. 6, No. 14, September 23, 1976.

Origins, Vol. 16, No. 36, 1987.

"Pacem in Terrus" (n. 143), 1963.

"The Church and Racism: Toward a More Fraternal Society."

U.S.C.C. "Policy Statement on Divestments, Disinvestments   and
South Africa"

U.S.C.C.'s "Statement on Portuguese Violations of Human   Rights in
its African Territories."

U.S.C.C.'s "Open-Letter to Henry Kissinger," April 7, 1976.

U.S.C.C.'s "Memo to the United States Senate Foreign Relations
Committee," June 1985.

U.S.C.C.'s "Statement on South Africa," October 16, 1985.

U.S.C.C.'s "Congressional Testimony on "U.N. Sanctions   Against
Rhodesia," Fall, 1973.

U.S.C.C.'s "Letter to Senate Foreign Relations Committee,   June 10,
1988.

UMC's United Methodist Information, May 9, 1975.

UMC's "Social Policy Statements and Recommended Actions,"
December 1988.

UMC's "Statement for the 1989-1992 Quadrennium," September
          1989.

UMC's "Social Policy Statements and Recommendations, 1968- 1969."

U.C.C. Pamphlet "To Aid UNITA: The Churches in Angola   Speak,"
November 11, 1985.

U.C.C.'s Lawrence Henderson, "Letter from Angola," January   19, 1986.

WNA, February 1975.

WNA, July 1975.

WNA, October 1975.

WNA, March 1976.

WNA, Spring 1977.

WNA, Summer 1977.

WNA, Spring 1978.

WNA, Summer 1978.

WNA, Spring 1979.

WNA, Summer 1979.

WNA, 1979/1980.

WNA, Summer 1980.

WNA, Winter 1980/81.

WNA, Summer 1981.

WNA, Summer 1982.

WNA, Spring 1983.

WNA, Summer/Autumn 1983.

WNA, Spring/Summer 1984.

WNA, Autumn 1984.

WNA, Winter 1984.

WNA, Summer 1985.

WNA, Fall 1985.

WNA, Winter/Spring 1985.

WNA, Spring 1986.

WNA, Summer 1988.

U.S. GOVERNMENT DOCUMENTS

Congressional Quarterly, October 4, 1986.

Congressional Quarterly Almanac, Vol. XLII, 1986.

Department of State Bulletin, June 6, 1960.

Department of State Bulletin, Vol. LXXIV, No. 1912, February 16, 1976.

Hearings, 95th Congress, Senate Committee on Foreign Relations

Hearings, 95th Congress, House Committee on International Relations

Legislation on Foreign Relations, 1978-1979.

Legislation on Foreign Relations, 1983-1984.

Legislation on Foreign Relations, 1984-1985.

Presidential Documents, Vol. II, No. 5, Monday, December 22, 1975.

NEWSPAPERS AND MAGAZINES

The New York Times, May 21, 1960.

The New York Times, November 7, 1975.

The New York Times, December 19, 1975.

The New York Times, January 27, 1982.

The Washington Post, November 8, 1975.

The Washington Post, February 3, 1986.

The Washington Post, June 24, 1990.

Reader's Digest, October 1971.

Reader's Digest, November 1971.

"Transcript of Televised Interview, A Conversation with the President," CBS Special Report with Walter Cronkite, March 3, 1981.